Brutalist Paris

Nigel Green & Robin Wilson

Blue Crow Media

First published in the United Kingdom in 2023 by Blue Crow Media

Map data from OpenStreetMap
Design by Supergroup Studios
Printed by Generation Press
Published by Blue Crow Media

Printed in the UK by a carbon-neutral printer on recycled responsibly sourced paper.

Blue Crow Media
London, United Kingdom
bluecrowmedia.com
This book and other titles are available to purchase from bluecrowmedia.com.

ISBN 978-1-912018-73-4

Acknowledgements

Many people have assisted in the development of this project since 2016. For their time and generosity we would particularly like to thank Emmanuel Benet and family, Iwona Buczkowska, Stéphane Degoutin, Gérard Grandval (1930–2021), Chloé Parent and Serge Renaudie. We would like to thank our collaborators in various, related projects who have helped to promote and evolve our work: Jon Astbury, Ruth Bernatek, Flavie Caroukis, Iain Chambers, Frédéric Jagu, Camille Ondet, Gascia Ouzounian, James Upton, Warren & Mosley, Stephanie White and Robert Worby. We would like to thank the Bartlett School of Architecture for research support. For their patience, support and expertise we would like to thank Derek Lamberton and the team at Blue Crow Media. The bar *Aux Folies*, Belleville requires special mention as a place of recuperation and inspiration. We thank all of the residents, workers and fellow urban travellers who we encountered across Paris these past six years, for their tolerance, curiosity, advice and reflections, this book is dedicated to them.

Part 1

The brutalist 'figure' of an alternative Paris

This book has evolved from research initially conducted for the *Brutalist Paris Map* (2017), part of the range of architectural maps published by Blue Crow Media since 2015. It is for this reason that its organisation follows, in part, a geographic structure, with its main body of illustrations arranged as a zoning of Paris according to the principal concentrations of its brutalist architecture. We also preserve a memory of the map to keep in mind the importance of the act of travel, of urban journeys, in the formation of this project and how it is potentially received and taken on by the reader. Undoubtedly, the recent popularity of brutalist architecture manifested through online media has to do, not simply with a new appetite for architectural form and its photographic imagery, but also for urban adventure, for a desire to discover new and unknown itineraries in the city.

The project has developed as an integral exploration and understanding of architecture through image and text, as a collaborative work between myself and the photographer Nigel Green. We have visited almost all of the buildings together, some numerous times, and only a handful separately. Although there is an ostensible separation of authorship between image and text, the response of the book as a whole to the architectures we encountered is a work of dialogue and co-production. The photographic image constructs a discourse from its object - a discursive record and transformation of its architectural subject matter - and that discourse also permeates the subsequent production of text. We do not seek an illustrative relation between image and text, but rather the production of two parallel and interrelated theses of Parisian brutalism and of the journeys undertaken. Whilst the photographic component provides an extensive, general survey of the production of the period as a whole, the text necessarily develops a more selective interpretation of a smaller range of key works, across a range of different architectural practices. As a point of intersection between the two, we also provide for each building within the image sections of the book a notational and conceptualising caption, as a reflective and circumstantial response to both the encounter with the building's 'reality', and to its image.

On Twitter, Roland-François Lack, a film theorist and author of the website *Ciné-Tourist*, responded to our brutalist map by placing it alongside three other maps of Paris, writing, 'this will be my favourite place-specific map, except perhaps for these'. The others included an early 20th century map of Parisian quarries and a map of somebody's favourite Parisian bars: city-portraits of the cartographic past, projecting the Parisian substrata to its surface, and redrawing the Parisian metro according to a *liquid* project. Lack reveals how our project follows in a long history of extracting very particular itineraries within the Parisian, urban totality; generating new narratives of the city through the pursuit of professional preoccupations and personal desires.

For the French art theorist Louis Marin, all maps draw out - redact from the complex reality of the urban ground - an itinerary that is also an *other* city; in effect, a utopia. Marin writes, 'at the very moment I look at the map - when I follow with my finger the route of a road, a contour line, when I cross here and not there a frontier, when I jump from one bank to the other - at this moment a figure is extracted from the ground, the figure of a projected journey, even if it is an imaginary one, a dreamed one' (Marin, 1993, p.414).

The brutalist 'figure' that we extract and project from the Parisian 'ground' will emerge here with all the complexity intended in Marin's use of the term. We assemble a diverse body of architectural expression and intent, manifesting sometimes divergent priorities and approaches to the urban challenges of the period. Architectural historian Anthony Vidler has referred to brutalism as 'a beast of late modernism', whose emergence caused crises of description and categorisation in the critical responses to it in the early 1960s, being 'ambiguously torn', as he puts it, between 'craft ideology' and 'abstract form-making' (Vidler, 2014, p.47). Similarly, we understand brutalism to represent a contested phase in the technological drive of modernity, and one which still holds relevance for our current moment. Brutalism represents, in part, a continuation in the onward domination of life by technology and the machine, but which also attempted to reassert a material poetics, valuing qualities of the 'as-found' and the handmade, and which desired to establish platforms for new forms of human relations and communication. In returning to this moment we also bring questions to bear on our present, about the spaces we inhabit collectively, our perceptual response to, and role as agents within them.

Our record of Parisian brutalism necessarily develops as both an architectural, historical account and as an encounter with the buildings in their current state of use, maintenance, restoration and, in some cases, their ruination and destruction. It is constructed across the totality of the sites and structures encountered and researched, but also as a consequence of the journeys between these different architectural destination points. Conducting the documentation in short, intense periods of site-work, through rapid itineraries of urban travel, the quality of the *brut* (rawness) in our account of this strata of Parisian, material history also incorporates a sense of exposure to the contemporary, urban environment, through constant mobility across and encounter with the diversity of Paris itself.

To journey in search of the brutalist architecture of Paris is to traverse expansively from the centre to the limits and beyond of the Parisian *Périphérique* in all directions, to the new town zones of the 1960s and 70s. The brutalist period of Parisian architecture produced limited but important architectural interventions into the dense fabric of central Paris. However, it is experienced most powerfully as an architecture of peripheral urbanism, which involved an attempt to manifest wholly new and alternative Parisian environments: satellite cities of a new, *multi-polaire* solution to urban growth. The result was an often radical departure from the familiar, historical Paris, towards the establishment of multiple, satellite centres. For us, the idea that we are investigating and recording 'new' Parisian environments – to present an *other* Paris to the familiar one, an unknown city within the known – drove us to pursue the commission in the first place, and has also informed our returns to Paris to continue the process and to maintain it as an ongoing project.

The brutalist period of expansion continued the long, post-World War II reconstruction, expansion and modernisation of the *Grands Ensembles* mass housing projects and ZUPs (Priority Zones for Urbanisation). The design and conception phase of the *Grands Ensembles* began in the late 1940s, and involved many leading French, pre-war modernist architects, such as Eugène Beaudouin, Jean Ginsberg, Le Corbusier, Marcel Lods, Fernand Pouillon and Bernard Zehrfuss. The production scale of the *Grands Ensembles* reached more than 300,000 dwelling units per year by 1960 (Newsome, 2004). Some of the architects we include in the book spent periods of their early careers within the offices of these practitioners, and were thus exposed to production at this urban scale. For example, both Renée Gailhoustet and Jean Renaudie, architects of the reconstruction of the centre of Ivry-sur-Seine (1968–87), worked within the atelier of Marcel Lods.

Architectural critic Jacques Lucan describes the brutalist phase of architecture in France as one of 'crisis'; that its poetics of material expression and form emerged as a reactionary response to the monotony of the system-built architecture of the earlier developments and the received discourse of modernity (Lucan, 1989). However, as with the earlier modernism, the work of the brutalist architects was also inevitably tied to the economic and technological evolutions within the construction sector and had to respond to, and in some cases evolve, the available techniques of construction appropriate to the task of building at scale. Notably, therefore, both Lucan and Vidler raise the condition of crisis in relation to brutalism, as a questioning of the rationale, means and categorisation of architectural production. In this way, brutalism functions as a form of 'critical architecture'. Indeed, the French architectural theorist Hélène Jannière explains how the etymology of the word criticism combines the Greek words *krinein* (judicial judgement) and *krisis*, linking criticism to crisis, as 'a moment of disciplinary reform and a moment of reform of the discourse' (Jannière, 2010, p.42).

Another vital part of the equation that contributed to the level of endeavour, innovation and critique within the architecture of the period was the involvement of a potent, leftist politics in the urbanism of the 1960s and 70s, and, indeed, the monetary power of the French Communist Party (PCF). Most importantly, this translated into local governance in the form of the communist-led departments and municipalities of outer Paris, the so-called *banlieues-rouge*, or 'red-belt', which reached a peak of communist control in the mid 1970s. Communist party subscription funded one of the most experimental and complex, late modern, brutalist buildings of central Paris, the Communist Party Headquarters (1980). Communist municipalities oversaw all of the radical social housing, administrative, cultural and major town centre urbanism in the sites of our itinerary in Aubervilliers, Bobigny, Clamart, Ivry, La Courneuve, Nanterre, Pantin, Saint-Denis and Saint-Ouen. Many of the architects employed were themselves communist party members.

Urban historian Kenny Cupers has charted the evolution of the *Grands Ensembles* with a particular emphasis on the increasing importance placed on the production of architecture and public space through user participation in the later projects. This was grounded in a growing desire on the part of architects and urban planners (informed by a theoretical base in the social sciences) to respond in a more comprehensive way to the contribution of occupants in the production of space. He writes, 'users were increasingly conceptualised not only as passive consumers of dwelling units but also as active constituents of the urban environments provided for them' (Cupers, 2010, p.117). This movement toward a performance of architecture as part of a wider set of contextual urban and societal principles, and in conjunction with the desire to create innovative architectural forms capable of establishing new and distinctive centres of urban development, are among the essential drives informing the nature of the architecture we encountered.

Part 2

Contemporary influences; traversing Paris *brut*

A recent example of urban travel writing by Parisian writer Eric Hazan shares some important locations with our brutalist mapping. Hazan's book *A Walk Through Paris: A Radical Exploration* (2018) recounts a journey across the city from the southerly Ivry-sur-Seine to the centre of Saint-Denis in the north. Although not an architectural survey, as such, Hazan begins with an interview with architect Renée Gailhoustet in Ivry, where she still lives in the *Le Liégat* phase of the town centre reconstruction, and concludes his journey at her town centre reconstruction adjacent to the Basilica-Cathedral of Saint-Denis. Between, Hazan traces a diverse and intimate history through architectural and topographic encounters across the centre of Paris. Significantly, there is also a potent project and projection in Hazan's work, a political and social one which undoubtedly resonates with that of Gailhoustet and her collaborators. Hazan claims that, although the corporate dominated museumification of central Paris has continued apace, the vitality of a working-class city persists at the margins and beyond the *Périphérique*; that the centre is still largely materially intact and ready for 'reconquest' (Hazan, 2018, p.59). Hazan's utopian desire would be to see the demolition of the *Hôtel de Ville* and *Préfecture de Police* of the *Île de la Cité*, and their stones reassembled into 'housing and community facilities' for all. He does not directly suggest that this new, collective centre should adopt an architecture on the lines of Gailhoustet's (he is enthusiastic about Ivry, but less so about Saint-Denis). However, in the structure of his book, his journey, the implication is there. For Hazan, the centre of the capital has been emptied, made void by neoliberal forces, but the new Parisian, satellite centres of the *banlieues* present more hopeful social and architectural possibilities for the future.

Another prolific source of urban representation of the expanded Paris of the late 20th century is that of film and television production. Examples of films which include references to our brutalist itinerary are numerous and include Pierre Granier-Deferre's adaptation of the Georges Simenon novel *Le Chat*, 1971, which features *Les Damiers* (the *quartier Louis-Blanc*) of Michel Folliasson in Courbevoie to the west; *Le Péril Jeune* (1994) by Cédric Klapisch and its reflections on Martin van Treeck's *Les Orgues de Flandre* in the 19th *arrondissement*; and Olivier Nakache and Éric Toledano's comedic, social drama *Tellement Proches* (2009) which is in part set within *Les Choux de Créteil* by Gérard Grandval. Notably, these are all examples of the more recognisable, signature architectures of the period; architectures of exuberant form and urban profile, reflected in their popular, adopted nomenclatures (of 'chequerboards', 'organs' and 'cabbages'). Architecture functions in these quite diverse examples of filmic, social realism as enigmatic signifiers of modernity and of a changing Paris of new and emergent identities. The earliest film, *Le Chat*, charts the moment of the earlier phase of urban demolition, redevelopment and the rehousing of populations that gave rise to the brutalist projects of modern renewal in the first place. At this film's location the story has come full circle, with *Les Damiers* currently suffering a slow decanting of its residents and demolition in preparation for a proposed, super-scaled redevelopment by Foster + Partners for the property corporation Hermitage Group – a vacuous new 'gateway' to *La Défense* of twin towers and podium.

The filmic depiction of the outer regions of Paris is a vast topic in its own right, and not containable here. However, during the period of our research on Paris we were drawn to the long-running police procedural and criminal justice drama, *Engrenages* (2005–21), retitled as *Spiral* for audiences in the UK. The urban locations of *Engrenages*, the scenes of crime, criminals' dwellings and home turf are almost uniquely peripheral and, indeed, in the sites of much of the northern sectors of Parisian brutalism – Pantin, Aubervilliers, La Courneuve, Saint-Denis. Sometimes the trajectory of a pursuit by car or by metro traverses a number of these areas. In an episode of series six there is a glimpse of Renée Gailhoustet's mixed-use development of the *Cité de la Maladrerie*, Aubervilliers as the police team head out in their car to Saint-Denis police station to begin an enquiry – an area which had been described previously in the series as 'like the Wild West' (*Engrenages*, 2017). It appears at the end of a street, *rue Lopez et Jules Martin*, looking north along the street façade of an earlier, rectilinear modern block (probably of the late 1950s or 60s) to a section of Gailhoustet's design that bridges across the street. The earlier, modern block sets the kind of visual urban frame more typical of the *Engrenages* peripheral film locations: anonymous, neglected, with the black grills of projecting balconies and stains on its concrete render making this façade look particularly industrial and decrepit. Beyond, Gailhoustet's bridge creates an urban horizon of complexity, its series of projecting, triangular forms create (in the brief moment that it is glimpsed in-frame) a crown of incomprehensible urban form, as if representative of a yet greater

threat of unknown urbanism to come, as the police team head out eagerly into the 'wilds'. In many ways, this is the perfect presentation of the spectacular, mediatised form of brutalist architecture: an architecture of shock that remains remote and incommensurable; a gateway to an unknown city, of dark interests.

There is something more to reflect on in relation to our brutalist interests within *Engrenages* than the crude, implied connection between crime and the modern, peripheral housing zones. There is something in the often melodramatic rawness of the characters of *Engrenages* - of police teams and criminal justice professionals always pushed to the limits, the trials of the city stretching them to dysfunction. The historic city in some series of *Engrenages* is a mere blur, a myth which serves no function, which the characters have no time for. Paris becomes an environment of wastelands (a quite unromanticised return of the *terrain-vague*), building sites, anonymous motels, ruins of light industry, anonymous suburban streets and housing estates. Whilst our experience of traversing the city to its brutalist, outer limits did not include extensive exposure to criminality, it did bring a disorienting exposure to an expanded city that was, in many of its parts, in crisis due to migration and subject to impressive demographic transformation. This we witnessed most powerfully in the migrant tent city of *avenue de Flandre*, outside van Treeck's aforementioned *Orgues* of *Îlot Riquet* in 2016; and then its displacement to the northern end of the *canal Saint-Martin* by 2018. New migration, as we heard firsthand from residents at *Cité de la Maladrerie*, Aubervilliers in 2018 had led to rapid increase in the turnover of new residents into the quarter and sense of greater disconnection and instability within the once more settled working-class community which had been the original beneficiary of the improvements to living conditions offered by Gailhoustet's development.

The temptation is to draw too easy an association between urban crisis and the architecture of outer Paris, of which the architecture of the brutalist period is often its most emblematic and memorable. However, the opposite is often the case. The brutalist era of social housing and new town construction could be said to be a last, monumental effort of state-financed placemaking, of the construction of civic space, and with an architectural ambition commensurate with those older values of inclusive, modern urban space before the onset of a corporate dominated, late-capitalist city. It could be argued that projects such as those of Renaudie and Gailhoustet at Ivry, Aubervilliers and Saint-Denis mark an apotheosis of the integration of architecture with urbanism, in an exhaustive effort of design to evolve complex, unique and stimulating living environments for all.

Our method of recording based on the general survey and the hectic itineraries of short visits necessitated a portrait of this period of Parisian architecture largely from the outside. For the most part, we capture the external, iconic image of the architecture of our itinerary. As, effectively, architectural tourists, we cannot, of course, speak of an experience of the architecture as inhabitants of the interior life of these new habitats for Parisian life. The life of the interior is fundamental to the innovations of many of the designs of the period, and their intentions and achievements cannot be fully grasped without recourse to this dimension. This we witnessed emphatically in visits to apartments in the Jean Hachette phase of Renaudie's Ivry-sur-Seine town centre reconstruction; to the offices and apartment of architect Iwona Buczkowska at her *Cité Les Longs Sillons* in the north of Ivry; and in gaining access to such public buildings as Jacques Kalisz's Administrative Centre of Pantin (now the National Centre of Dance), and Jean Peccoux's Gymnasium Jules Ladoumègue.

These moments of more complete access were the exception rather than the rule. However, as travellers within the urban conditions that surround and interpenetrate the brutalist sites – in their public spaces, undercrofts and adjacent streets – we can also validly offer more than just a sterile, architectural portrait of external form, and have aimed to report back a more expansive impression of the terms of brutalism's contact, or, indeed, *contract*, with wider Paris. As well as making portraits of buildings as urban objects, we also inhabit and study the spatial 'inter-zones' and thresholds of transition from the 'older' or 'normative' urban order to the spaces of proposed architectural, brutalist 'difference', and seek to understand their intervention into, or reinvention of, the Parisian context.

PORT

Centre
(within the *Périphérique*)

Conference Hall, UNESCO
Marcel Breuer, Pier Luigi Nervi, Bernard Zehrfuss, 1958
'Not only bones, but bones, muscles and skin combined.'
- Marcel Breuer, 1955
30 October 2016, pm: views from the perimeter; rain chains and the storm gully, a *brut* movement of water.

Maison du Brésil
Le Corbusier and Lúcio Costa, 1959
A 'medieval complication of supports'. – G.E. Kidder Smith, 1961
28 October 2016, pm: the foyer: colour-stained concrete projections; the glass mailbox (a diaphanous *Unité* in miniature).

303 304 306 307 313 315 316

Telecommunications Building

Pierre Vivien, 1970

Objet trouvé; a prototype to scale 1 : 10. The garden of perpetual drought.

Fire Station Headquarters and Barracks

Prvoslav Popovic and Jean Willerval, 1973

Caserne; utopic ship of *sapeurs*. A thesis of rounded tectonics. *Brut* dialogue with topography; the slipway of boulevard Masséna.

SAPEURS-POMPIERS
DE PARIS

Les Olympiades Towers

Michel Holley, Jean Chaillet, André Martinat and Michel Proux, 1974

'On the other side the rain rears up on the boulevards of a big city...' - André Breton, 1932

29 October 2016, pm: hostile gaze on the long ramps of *Esplanade Olympiades*.

Office/Residence Mouzaïa
Claude Parent and André Remondet, with poet Catherine Val, 1974
29 October 2016, pm: the 'Bureau of Negation': a *brut*-picturesque.
The articulated flesh of architecture.

Tour de Mars

Henry Pottier and Michel Proux, 1974

30 October 2016, pm: Mars; research among the brutal bases of *Îlot Cassiopée*.

Ternes Postal Centre
Jean Dumont, 1975
30 November 2021, pm: aggregate textures and moss, the low barrier of *rue Poncelet*: vertical views to a glacial landscape.

35
orange

Tour Totem

Michel Andrault and Pierre Parat,
with artist Yvette Vincent-Alleaume, 1978

30 October 2016, pm: western winds on the podium of the future.

Australian Embassy
Harry Seidler with Marcel Breuer and Pier Luigi Nervi, 1978
Polysemic pilotis: screen and concrete pneumatics: borrowed remains from a bastion of the future.

Communist Party Headquarters

Oscar Niemeyer with Paul Chemetov, Jean Deroche and Jean Prouvé, 1980

The ground plane as plinth and elevation; horizontal portal to the new society.

Les Orgues de Flandre (Îlot Riquet)

Martin Schultz van Treeck, 1973 and 1980

Contortions of a new *Cité Radieuse*; universal views to the street.

29 October 2016, am: the migration crisis; a tent city, *avenue de Flandre*.

ACTING

LIBERTÉ
ÉGALITÉ
FRATERNITÉ
COLLÈGE
GERMAINE TILLION

The Germaine Tillion College

Claude Parent, 1987

Layered rustication; a façade of intaglio incision.
Entrance as performative hinge.

Part 3

Definitions: from the core to the peripheries of the *brut*

The project began, and still grapples with, a question of definitions, the establishing of the identity or criteria for brutalist buildings and how, in our case, to transfer a certain historical understanding and experience of brutalism from the UK context (British buildings, British criticism), to the Parisian one. An entirely consistent categorisation of Parisian brutalism is not possible; at least, not one that incorporates over 50 examples from across more than two decades of architectural production, as we do here. Moreover, the word brutalism is not in common usage in French architectural circles (although it has been more consistently used in the French architectural press in recent years). It is often deemed superfluous, offering no useful differentiation of this later period of modernism of the 1960s to early 1980s from earlier, modernist production. Some French architects, such as Serge Renaudie, go as far as to qualify it as a term of abuse (Chambers, 2021). One can understand how it ostensibly runs contrary to the notions of societal care and collective hope invested in the design and programming of much architecture of the period.

To encourage a greater acceptance and consideration of the term within French architectural culture is certainly not the aim of this publication. However, the use of the term in this context does offer the opportunity to bring a different set of parameters through which to observe, compare and differentiate the diversity of production during the period. This can be a valuable exercise, as long as it does not simply remain at the level of categorisation (the classification of types and of hierarchies of the pure and impure), but which seeks to establish the grounds for more critical questions to emerge regarding the desires and achievements of the period across the diversity of its production, and how these questions might also bear upon the present conditions of the city's evolution.

An online image search for Parisian brutalism reveals a somewhat chaotic patchwork of buildings from the second half of the 20th century, a rather uncertain candidature of brutalist examples driven by different agents: individual, urban explorers; architects; commercial practices (such as Zupagrafika models); art practices (such as that of Laurent Kronental, who has photographed elderly residents of Parisian brutalism in-situ for his series, *Souvenir d'un Futur*). As our work was always to be, in part, disseminated through these channels, we decided that our framework definition of brutalism needed to be responsive to the aggregate of definitions found here, as well to those of received architectural, historical sources.

For the latter, we necessarily returned to critic Reyner Banham's definitions of brutalism within his essay of December 1955 in *The Architectural Review*, entitled 'The New Brutalism'. We encounter there a quite fluid set of terms, aesthetic genealogies and qualifications, almost exclusively directed to establish the brutalist credentials of the work of a single architect: the British practice of Alison and Peter Smithson. Significantly, this originating thesis of brutalism was not conceived with recourse to the medium of concrete, but through the steel frame and panel system construction of the Smithsons' Hunstanton School in Norfolk (1954), on which Banham published a separate building report, which also introduced the building in manifesto-like terms alongside a technical report. Concrete dominates the material palette of our itinerary, with the exception of aspects of the work of Jacques Kalisz, especially his Nanterre School of Architecture, *La Défense* (1971) - a remarkable metal frame and panel construction designed in collaboration with Roger Salem, but now a ruin awaiting possible restoration and repurposing.

Banham's Hunstanton School report also emphases the presence of a deep rigour and ethics of material use, with 'every element truly what it appears to be, serving as necessary structure and necessary decoration'. This demands of the architect, as Banham asserts, 'an existential responsibility [...] for every brick laid, every joint welded, every panel offered up' (Banham, 1954, p.149). Clearly this is a level of attention way beyond the scope of most individual architects operating at the economies of scale necessary in the late modern period of brutalist urbanism in Paris. However, it usefully articulates how brutalism entails a desire for a closer integration of the technical and the artistic, the constructional and the poetic. Such qualities do surface in the Parisian, brutalist story, in its different circumstances of material technologies and labour, and in more piecemeal, fragmentary modes, rather than as a totalising ethos.

We draw on the historical manifesto writing and debates on the origins of brutalism in the post-war era as grounds for a critical *inclusion* of diverse examples, rather than for the creation of a purest framework. After all, the 'New Brutalism' essay itself drew on and defined a broad span of expression across visual art and spatial production, including the art and curatorial work of the Independent Group (which included the Smithsons, photographer Nigel Henderson and sculptor Eduardo Paolozzi), principally their exhibition *The Parallel of Art and Life* at the Institute of Contemporary Art (1953). In more purely architectural terms, the 'New Brutalism' article is perhaps better understood as a discursive frame or vehicle for Banham's criticism at that time, a temporary scaffolding erected in the episodic activities of journal criticism and then discarded when the focus of Banham's critical allegiances shifted. However, Banham does provide a set of working principles for identifying brutalist buildings, such as the occasion requires, and which transfers across different materials and techniques of construction: the 'memorability' and, indeed, the 'ruthlessness' of the spatial system as image (that is, the clarity of a building's visual identity, and formal legibility as a programme); the 'clear exhibition of structure'; and 'the valuation of materials "*as found*"' (which, in the earlier building report on Hunstanton, Banham specifically identifies with Dadaist sensibilities) (Banham, 1955).

Raised less precisely within that nexus of values was also a general propensity toward 'primitive' or essential material expression, in the association of the term *béton brut* (raw concrete) adopted from Le Corbusier, to *Art Brut* and the French critic Michel Tapié's related notion of *une Art Autre*. In this, the 'New Brutalism', in its attempt to master aesthetic production across disciplines, shares an important seam of aesthetic concerns with earlier post-war debates within French culture. Art historian Steven Harris describes a common project between Tapié, the critic Charles Estienne and the leading surrealist poet and essayist André Breton to articulate a way beyond pre-war surrealism and Dadaism, toward a fusion of surrealism and the new abstract expressionism (Harris, 2004). This latter implied a reassertion of, what Harris terms, the 'sovereign individual' within the creative process, a reclaiming of ground against the formlessness and negation of Dadaist expression toward an intuitive, spontaneous abstraction, which also validated individual agency and signature. Interestingly, this was in part argued for, on the part of Breton and Estienne in particular, through a revival of interest in pre-classical forms of French artistic expression. This constituted an 'atavistic leap' back, as Harris puts it, involving an interest in the ancient coins of the Gaulish period, as representative of a culture of gestural expression, similarly hovering between the figurative and the abstract (Harris, 2004, p.203). Although expressed and applied through different terms of reference and context, such oscillation between the modern and the pre-modern, the figurative and the abstract, the individual and the collective is a consistent characteristic of the creative, spatial practices we encountered across brutalist Paris, in the channelling of the advanced aesthetic syntheses of the period toward the creation of art and architectural expressions for a new French society.

There are also wider issues and longer histories of aesthetic categorisation to be untangled within the founding expressions of brutalism and their discursive contexts. Australian architectural historian John Macarthur makes the point that Banham's articles in this period were published within the wider frame of a set of editorial campaigns in *The Architectural Review* from the 1930s onwards, which championed, through diverse and sometimes contradictory forms of expression, the revival of 18th century aesthetics of the picturesque, as the basis of a renewed urban aesthetic of dynamic contradistinctions. While Banham's declared stance was to reject *The Architectural Review*'s concerns for the picturesque as a parochial reaction to modernity, Macarthur reminds us that a broader understanding of the spectrum of the picturesque as inclusive of a theory of ugliness and disgust would position brutalism as an extension to the picturesque as a longer philosophical reflection on material aesthetics. Within the context of this programme of aesthetic reflection on the tensions between new forms of post-war modernity and, broadly speaking, romanticism, Macarthur defines brutalism as a form of '*hard picturesque*' which is aesthetically challenging, 'and the denunciation of a soft sentimental picturesque in the name of a rigorous and truthful architecture' (Macarthur, 2000, p.263).

One would have to concede that with the arrival of projects like the brutalist map series, and the abundant appreciation of brutalist architecture on social media, its status as 'hard' aesthetic is itself transitioning, or has already transitioned toward something more 'familiar'; that brutalism has lost its shock value, its inherent material and aesthetic force of critique, as antithesis to dominant, 'soft', aesthetic sensibilities. However, this also signals a moment at which we can reassess the impact of the work of the period and to begin a process of more acute differentiation within the common categorisation.

One prominent, online example that we do not include in our survey is the work of Spanish architect Ricardo Bofill, and his housing complexes of *Abraxas*, Noisy-le-Grand (1982) and the *Arcades du Lac* (1981) in Saint-Quentin-en-Yvelines. Bofill's work attains effortlessly to the kind of mediatised spectacle of architectural representation characteristic of the online array of brutalism, portrayed with particular power in the work of Laurent Kronental. Bofill's work shares a scale, exuberance of form-making and some of the constructional systems with the architectures of our itinerary. However, Bofill also clearly adopts postmodern tendencies in the development of the façade that eliminate almost all recourse to the 'ethics' or 'honesty' of material use and exposition of structural performance.

It is not that we can claim absolute rigour or unity of purpose in this regard for all the examples we include. However, Bofill's façades are explicitly structured through an ambiguous play of borrowed and modified historical, architectural elements, characteristic of postmodernism; a screen-like representational slippage between monumental, three-dimensional mouldings of structural parts, through to the purely surface effects of motifs in thin relief. Brutalism applied to Bofill's work in Paris could *only* be levelled as a term of abuse: the brutality of the disjunction between the human occupants and the architecture they inhabit, which the repertoire of neoclassical motifs only seems to amplify and make more gratuitous. Bofill's artful architectural games at scale serve to reinforce a sense of the domination of specialists (architects, urbanists, town planners) over the lives of individuals, as subjects to a bad utopianism of the 'inhuman' and the 'absurd' to recall critic Robert Hughes castigation of the new French urbanism of the period in the BBC TV series *Shock of the New*.

Hughes was in fact directing his ire at buildings by different architects on the other side of Paris at the time. Those specific terms of attack accompanied a panning shot across an area of Nanterre/La Défense, which included large-scale housing projects by Émile Aillaud and Jacques Kalisz. Aillaud's *Cité Pablo Picasso* – now commonly known as the *Tours Aillaud* or *Tours Nuages* – was the particular focus of Hughes's critique, and which he judged with an invective that only a sweeping, polemic overview of modernist, urban history could generate, describing it as 'a piece of social scar tissue - gimmicky, condescending, Alphaville modernism' (Hughes, 1980).

We include the *Cité Pablo Picasso* here as example of Aillaud's work, not because we can offer a precise counter thesis to Hughes's polemic critique of their social and environmental impact, but because of their clearer credentials as late modernist works, that deliver a specific, strategic evolution of the more reductive principles of earlier modernism, rather than the kind of rejection of it evident in Bofill's architecture. The spectacular nature of form and the volumetric effects of the *Tours Nuages*, as single, or melded clusters of cylindrical forms, proceeds from a desire on Aillaud's part for a mass housing design that departs from the rectangular, cellular mode of modernist housing provision, to provide multi-aspect, dual-orientated apartments of a more organic and irregular conception. In this sense, the forms of the *Tours Nuages* express with integrity the dominant programmatic aim of the design, and also relate to other housing projects within our itinerary, such as Grandval's *Les Choux de Créteil*.

As architectural monuments and urban image the *Tours Nuages* clearly have the capacity to elicit a powerful, visual impression that goes beyond any purely architectural specification. It would be insufficient to judge that Banham's 'memorability' of image had collapsed purely into gimmickry here, even if one does happen to find the *Cité Pablo Picasso* an offence to architectural sensibilities. Their 'image' is ambiguous, both somehow playful and threatening; intricate and generous at the level of detail and yet also exuding a certain megalomania of gigantism; a colourful citadel and an *îlot* of otherness.

The towers' mosaic surfaces by Laurence Aillaud (daughter of Émile) and her partner, the artist Fabio Riéti, are one of the great endeavours of the integration of architecture and public art of the period: the creation of a total environment of *pâte de verre*, urban mosaic. This has its own, particular material quality that one more commonly encounters on a much smaller scale and in the interior (a wall, a sill, a table). On the day that we visited, we arrived immediately after a sustained downpour, and the *cité* could be imagined as a huge wet room enclosure for the gigantic, mosaic snakes that coil through its *aires de jeux* (play spaces). The disjunction between monumental, architectural form and the individual scale of the mosaic piece is one which continually intervenes into the impression of the towers at close hand. Between these two dizzyingly different registers of scale, there is an 'intermediary' scale created by the tower's window frames. These comprise the three permutations of the celebrated, bespoke fenestration by Aillaud, of round, tear-shaped and square with rounded corners.

Fenestration typically introduces the human scale into the urban image; and in viewing a tower block from a distance one usually perceives, more-or-less precisely, its subdivision into units of living space. However, with the *Tours Nuages* the subdivision and the scale of apartments is entirely masked by the uniform application of the mosaic. Therefore, although the human scale aperture is beautifully expressed here, the spatial system and the density of occupation to which it relates remains entirely mysterious. One might speculate (in the mode of Georges Perec), on the possibility that one tower has a single occupant whilst another has as many occupants as windows. The towers may plausibly contain monumental spiral staircases to rooftop observatories; or house a yet more fantastical, helicoidal system of staircases that serve an elaborately categorised library on many hundreds of levels. In short, there is an abstraction of scale here, which might give rise to impressions of whimsy and the daydream, or equally might reinforce a sense of urban alienation.

A cause to, perhaps, perceive more threat than whimsy in the symbolic, urban image of the *Tours Nuages* occurred to me on *rue du Faubourg Saint-Martin*, whilst looking at the shop front of the *Armurerie de la Gare de l'Est*, with its own quite remarkable mosaic skin from the late 1950s. There, within its considerable array of fatal weaponry, was a heavy machine gun, reminiscent of the types used in World War II. I was struck by the resemblance between the characteristic, cylindrical, perforated barrel jacket of this weapon and the smooth, fenestrated cylinders of Aillaud's towers. The memory of munitions and warfare is of course further amplified by the camouflage-like colour combinations of their variegated mosaic.

Viewed at a distance, Aillaud and Riéti's mosaics still retain the power and nuance of their intervention into the skyline of Nanterre. However, up close, the effects of weathering and water ingress are evident, with sections of mosaic missing and some clumsily refilled with concrete render. The towers are currently the subject of studies for recladding by the French architects Agence RVA (Renaud Vignaud and Associates), for whom the preferred solution is a new, metal skin of pixelated colouration. Such actions of renewal can never be exclusively directed at the aesthetic integrity of the original design. RVA's solution for the outer cladding addresses a quite different set of criteria for thermal performance to Aillaud's original specification, in order for the towers to comply with contemporary building standards for housing. We can only wait to see the effects of RVA's solution applied at scale. However, based on the firm's project imagery there is a considerable danger that the new cladding will bring the aesthetics of the towers into greater conformity with the metal and glass, corporate architectures of the nearby La Défense. This highlights how the complex integration within architectural production of the available technologies, its economies of labour, its social thesis and commissioning brief contributes to the limits and possibilities for aesthetic endeavour within any given historical moment, and which is a value beyond replication in the present. What is very unlikely to be preserved in any work of renewal is the power of the *Tours Nuages* in their symbolic ambiguity as urban objects and the value of their qualities of alterity, the principal criterion for their inclusion in a compendium of Parisian *brut*.

Part 4

The brutalist construction site

Within a purely architectural pursuit of the 'as-found', the apprehension and expression of the conditions of the building site, the moment of assemblage, is paramount; that is, the creation of a material expression at the intersection of labour and the medium of construction. Architectural historian Adrian Forty provides a diverse discussion of the 'discourse of concrete' in the modern and late modern periods as a combination of the trace of both the 'primitive and the sophisticated' in the dialogue between engineering or 'system' and its execution (Forty, 2012, p.127).

The term *béton brut* itself derives originally from an item of correspondence by Le Corbusier and describes the material finish of his later works in the post-World War II period, particularly the *Unité d'Habitation* in Marseilles

(1952). Whilst the notion of the material finish 'as found' has come to define brutalism within the current understanding of the canon, and even traced back to William Morris, craft revival and the authentic expression of materials, it was more so a product of the conditions of the building site, the fact that there were multiple contractors working on the *Unité*'s construction, with different levels of skill. Le Corbusier wrote, 'there were eighty contractors and such a massacre of concrete that there was no way of imagining how to construct useful relationships through rendering. I had decided: leave everything "brut"' (Vidler, 2014, p.46).

A similar material discourse is in evidence at Le Corbusier's *Maisons Jaoul* in western Paris, Neuilly-sur-Seine (1955), the earliest building included in the book. For this pair of family houses, inspired by the barrel roof construction of Mediterranean vernacular architecture, a radically 'raw' deployment of materials was specified. The trace of the making hand is discernible in the cementing of the brick joints, the working of the exposed sections of the concrete slab (producing an expression of the barrel roof profile and of the lower floor slabs on the end elevations, like a section cut). However, Forty notes that there is a level of contradiction between means and ends at the *Maisons Jaoul* in relation to materials, in that the brickwork was executed by a skilled and experienced craftsman, but who was instructed to conduct the work with a loose hand; and that a less experienced contractor for the concrete made a particularly bad job of the first-floor concrete slab and then overcompensated with a very precise and crisp moulding of the roof slab (Forty, 2012). Paris-based architectural critic and historian Andrew Ayers records how similar strategies were applied to the brickwork, with a relay of different brick layers taking over every three courses (Ayers, 2004, p.306). The loose hand of the skilled, the overcompensation of the less capable; a now largely indecipherable material and ideological dialogue between precision and accident, restraint and excess, across the professional classes of design and construction.

The work of Paul Bossard for the housing complex of *Les Bleuets*, Créteil (1962) could be understood to express something approximate to Le Corbusier's treatment of materials at the *Maisons Jaoul*, transferred to the context of mass housing. Forty, also makes interesting observations here about the logic of construction. For, with *Les Bleuets* (The Cornflowers, which, as with many of the names of the new developments, is probably a reference to previous land use) there is a combination of the handmade with the precast panel system. Forty explains that Bossard evolved this design from his student diploma project and, against the norms of professional roles within the French building industry, undertook to design the precast system himself and oversee in detail its assemblage on-site (Forty, 2012, p.249). Large pieces of shale, embedded in the roughly textured concrete panels at the outer surfaces of the plinth and the floor slabs, were placed by the construction workers at the site whilst the concrete was still wet, with the variability of skill in this process of rapid, 'primitive' *appliqué* embraced as a part of the material ethos of the project.

Notably, the aforementioned Agence RVA, which worked on the renovation of *Les Bleuets* (completed in 2019), describes Bossard's work as being among the most 'legible examples' of French brutalism, which it ascribes to its 'simple use of raw materials without artifice' (Agence RVA, 2019). Arguably, though, there *is* artifice at work in Bossard's assemblage and combination of materials, which also interestingly tests Banham's array of brutalist criteria. The treatment of the horizontal, structural layers of the blocks amount to an artisanal rustication of the façade, but this is also conceptual, for it *connotes* a material effect beyond its actual constructional and material reality. The rustication achieves the effect of a rugged, almost geological sense of connection to the ground, as if the blocks had been assembled atop 'found' masonry plinths, or assembled intuitively with masonry techniques of older, local origin. This would seem to place it beyond the strict conception of material integrity in Banham's terms. However, it is precisely this 'artifice' of materials that contributes to its 'memorability as image'. The instincts of the brutalist sensibility in evidence here are not to dispense with artifice as such, but to generate, from its renewed poetic attention and artisanal engagement with raw materials and the resources of human labour, a material

experience and image of architecture that is both honest *and* transformative, rigorous and poetically charged with subtle fictions of context and connection to place.

As with their proposed work at Aillaud's *Cité Pablo Picasso*, Agence RVA's work at *Les Bleuets* reconfigures aspects of the façades and interiors to meet contemporary standards of accommodation and building performance. They have realised, as far as we could discern from our short period on site, a robust and apt renovation of the apartment blocks, in their replacing of fenestration, concrete panelling and the estate's coloured blinds in hues of green, yellow, orange and russet red. However, original photographs of *Les Bleuets* reveal how the current restoration also reduces the 'rawness' of the original palette of concrete, stone and wood. Whilst maintaining the same material components, RVA tones down its material variegation in favour of more standardised products and finishes. The original material performance of *Les Bleuets* staged a more powerful affront to the standardisation of earlier modernism, establishing its departure from the functionalist past in more emphatic terms, as a more bespoke, crafted inflection of a system-built architecture. This original variegation of material effect would have undoubtedly contributed to the visual impact, or 'memorability' of the 'image' of *Les Bleuets*, in Banham's terms, as an array of rectilinear blocks that have quite idiosyncratically taken on a primitive, organic and topographical character.

For the, perhaps, best known of the founding projects of Parisian brutalism we must return to Le Corbusier and his collaboration with Brazilian architect Lúcio Costa for the *Maison du Brésil* (1959), a student residence in the *Cité Internationale Universitaire*. The campus of the *Cité Universitaire* has the feel of a model village of uncertain scale, operating at a different pace, as a different pocket of city time. It is park-like, with a meandering route linking its national residences and their garden terrains. For our purposes, it offers an important transitional point between earlier, modernist principles of spatial composition and material use and the establishing of potentially 'brutalist' ones; or, it at least offers one way of articulating the terms of a shift between these two labels of architectural 'style' and the periods which they broadly designate. I refer to the proximity of two works by Le Corbusier here, for his *Fondation Suisse* (1931) is situated just a few hundred metres to the west of the *Maison du Brésil*.

In the years between the completion of the two, obvious material component changes occurred, registering a shift into different economies of production and labour in the post-World War II period. There are also important compositional changes which resonate with wider questions of urbanism and the relationship of the individual building to the city, played out here on the scale of the campus microcosm. The *Maison du Brésil* is almost exclusively a masonry building, of textured concrete, cast in-situ; aggregate, precast concrete panels; and an application of stone into sections of the concrete walls of the ground floor (a 'rubble masonry'). The outer metal frame and façade panelling of the earlier *Fondation Suisse* appears more refined, more 'advanced'; it resonates with material signifiers of progress and a 'purer', machined modernity of functionalism. In describing the two buildings in the early 1960s, architectural critic and photographer G.E. Kidder Smith writes of the 'bulkier' presence of the later *Maison du Brésil*, and also notes the differences in the way the two buildings meet the ground. He observes, 'the Brazilian Pavilion sits more heavily on the ground than the Swiss and has an awkward, almost medieval (the new Le Corbusier?) complication of supports'. Seemingly in contrast to the heavy expressions of mass and articulation of the pilotis, Kidder Smith also notes how the 'communal ground floor' evolves as 'a free shape rear projecting wing that "floats" under the main mass' (Kidder Smith, 1961, pp.82-83).

The *Fondation Suisse* is not without communal elements on the ground floor, but they are more compactly positioned beneath and to the rear of the building, allowing a front elevation of much greater simplicity and a ground plane which prioritises the pilotis and interspaces between them. At the *Fondation Suisse*, like the much larger *Unité* housing blocks of Le Corbusier, such as in Marseilles and Nantes-Rezé, we see a more definitive separation of the main block of accommodation from the ground, the pilotis serving as structural and symbolic device in this sense. 'By raising the building in this manner', wrote Nikolaus Pevsner, 'it becomes disconnected from the soil, a lighter species of matter' (Cherry and Pevsner, 2007, p.24). This we might understand as an expression, or even symptom, of its 'difference' as an architectural language; its radicalism and utopianism. As the American critic and theorist Fredric Jameson writes, 'the act of disjunction was violent, visible and had a very real symbolic significance – as in Le Corbusier's great pilotis, whose gesture radically separates the new utopian space of the modern from the degraded and fallen city fabric, which it thereby explicitly repudiates' (Jameson, 1991, pp.12–13).

With the brutalist *Maison du Brésil*, the act of symbolic separation from the ground persists as far as the principal accommodation block is concerned, but across the composition as a whole a more complex relation to the ground is in evidence. Certain aspects of the complex are emphatically expressed as grounded; reconnected to the city context, or, 're-soiled'. This occurs not simply through its greater tectonic bulk and in the 'cruder', more expressionistically jointed connection between the structural pilotis and the first-floor slab, but in the more expansive programmatic and representational role of the communal elements of the ground floor – the 'free shape' that Kidder Smith writes of. The form of the ground-floor spaces were, in part, the result of an intervention by the authorities of the *Cité Universitaire*, who wished the original orientation of the building by Costa to be reversed. Le Corbusier persuaded Costa to accommodate this reversal by an extensive reworking of the ground floor (Ayers, 2004, p.222).

This space extends out expansively from the main block of accommodation and has to be actively navigated in order to arrive at the centre of the building and its entrance. It projects an obstructive, almost defensive, rubble masonry wall out to the western edge of the residence's front garden. The plan of the *Maison du Brésil* reveals how the ground-floor volumes take on a quite contradictory disposition to the rectilinear block above, expressing a new plasticity of curvilinear form and irregular geometries; a disorienting flow of spatial compression and dilation which evolves as if uncontained beneath and beyond the limits of the pilotis space; as a new type of spatial agent that actively disturbs and distorts the received rules of the modern.

This reconnection with the ground and the complexity of the ground-floor volumes is accompanied by a studied, tectonic detail of the southern stairwell in elevation, which greets the visitor on the approach to the building's entrance. Here, through the intersection of vertical and horizontal apertures, and the exterior expression of the profile of the stairwell treads on the exterior, the point of contact between the ground-floor volume and the main housing block above is dramatised and made ambiguous, in a work of sculptural tectonics that stages a confusion between up and down; connection and disconnection. The stairwell registers from the exterior as a complex joint and spatial puzzle between the ground and the upper floors (see page 21, top image). This is one of the genuinely iconic details of the period: *brut*; intensely crafted yet also atavistic; a gesture to the pre-modern as *other*; and a plausible response to the hybridisation of the surreal and the abstract that Breton and Estienne desired.

It would seem that, in this post-war era, achieving the effect of a clear separation from ground is no longer symbolically viable, but that now a new symbolic activation of the ground plane takes hold. In contrast to the cellular accommodation block above, this irregular vessel of communal space is a searching, exploratory form, as if uncertain of its own limits. If this 're-soiling' of the *Unité* is also charged with a symbolic function, then perhaps it anticipates, or 'figures' (to recall Marin's terminology), the complexity of wider urban expansions to come in the post-war era (beyond the student enclave of the *Cité Universitaire*); and the requirement for new forms of architecture to intersect with a more complex urban, social thesis and conception of the 'public'.

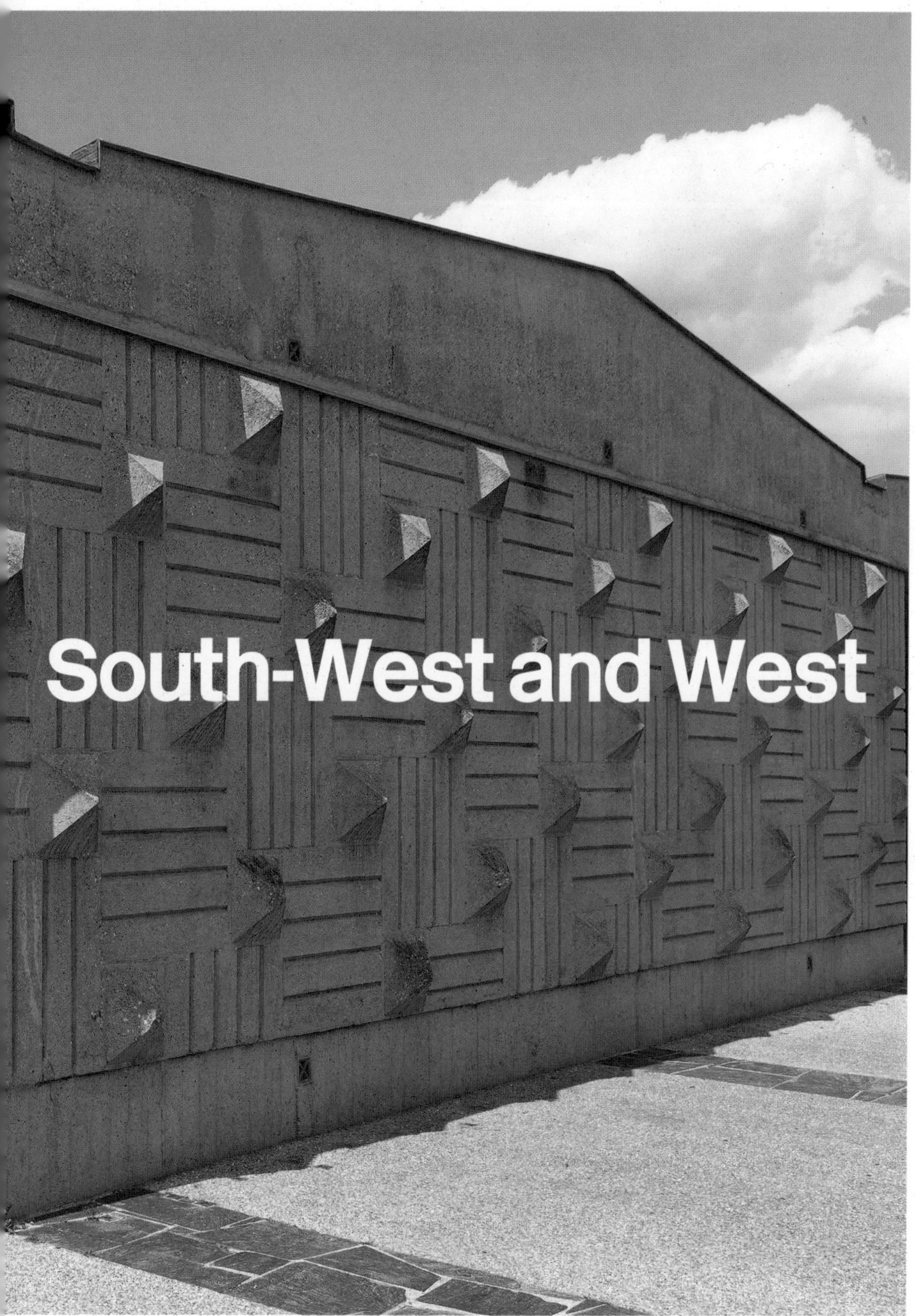

South-West and West

Intercommunal Cemetery

Robert Auzelle and Ivan Jankovic, 1956

Prismatic rustication; a universal façade.
Graveyard journey to the toilet block Diamanti.

Antoine Béclère Hospital
Henry Pottier and Jacques Vial
with artist/architect L'Œuf Centre d'Etudes, 1971
The water tower core: monumental ascent through pilotis.

The Little Round Library

Atelier de Montrouge, 1965

The municipal palisade: 'symbolic violence' against the *monument historique*.

21 May 2022, pm: moped repairs in the communal gardens, *rue de Champagne*.

Maisons Jaoul

Le Corbusier, 1955

Material ideologies of the *brut*: the 'loose hand' of the skilled artisan.

Nanterre School of Architecture

Jacques Kalisz and Roger Salem, 1971

Ruins of the future; a steel frame and plastic picturesque. 29 February 2020, pm: the sudden storm. A bullet through the street sign: '*Allée Le Corbusier*'.

Ecole d'Architecture de Paris-La Défense
41

Vision 80
Jean-Pierre Jouve, Andrei Frieschlander and Charles Mamfredos, 1973
A *Unité* cradled in dry dock: the sanitised undercroft and gated separation from the esplanade.

P
SAISONS

Les Damiers (The Chequerboards)

Michel Folliasson with Jacques Binoux, Abro and Henri Kandjian, 1976

Totemic playgrounds of the vertical city.

29 February 2020, pm: interior phase of demolition in process, eastern sector.

Tours Nuages, Cité Pablo Picasso

Émile Aillaud with Laurence Aillaud and Fabio Riéti, 1978

A weathered, urban mosaic/mosaic urbanism; utopic surfaces in fragmentation. Hughes's 'social scar tissue' diatribe, 1980.

Cœur

Sports Centre (Cercle Nautique de France)

Albert Grégoire, 1979

Rowing crews and the arrival of *La Dorade* (disembarkation of the remains of Napoleon).

Part 5

International collaboration; an experimental brutalism for the institutions of post-war Paris

The early phase of brutalism in Paris saw a number of important collaborations by international architects, some brought together as a result of migration, but also as a result of a desire for international collaboration in the establishing of important, post-war institutions. Of particular note in this regard is the collaboration of Marcel Breuer, a Hungarian-born architect, trained at the Weimar Bauhaus, the Italian engineer Pier Luigi Nervi and French architect Bernard Zehrfuss for the UNESCO headquarters (1958) in the 7th *arrondissement*. Notably, both Le Corbusier and Costa were part of the committee that reviewed the proposed design, along with other leading modernist architects and designers, Walter Gropius, Sven Markelius and Ernesto Rogers.

Our point of focus here is the trapezoidal, concertina-like Conference Hall, which saw the most important contribution of Nervi as engineer. (Nervi was also responsible for the pilotis of the principal building of the complex, the Secretariat, and its freestanding, concrete porch.) Despite Nervi having by this stage in his career developed a specialism for innovative precast concrete design, the structure for the Conference Hall was built from in-situ, formwork concrete and bears the marks of its shuttering. Nervi employed a single, corrugated or folded-plate, concrete shell, which allowed for the fusion of structure into the building envelope as a single entity (Calvo-Salve, 2018). The form is also visible in the interior, creating a longitudinal, ribbed roof scape of a more finessed, fluted and chamfered profile, and a backdrop to the auditorium stage that appears like a concrete curtain.

According to construction historian Javier Martín Fuentes, it was Breuer who persuaded Nervi that the corrugated structural form should be used for the façades of the east and west elevations, as well as the roof structure, thereby achieving the more complete integration of structural system within the architectural (Fuentes, 2018). Here, in the use of concrete as tensile building envelope, albeit for a relatively simple, single-volume form, the brutalist principles of structural and material expression and the legibility of the building as image are achieved with an unmatched economy, almost quite literally cut from a single cloth.

The Conference Hall sits behind the eight storey, Y-shaped, Secretariat and borders the site's western perimeter onto *avenue de Ségur*, from which the full, folded elevation is visible. It appears here as a precisely crafted, almost mechanistic form, with the suggestion that its folds are hinged, and with kinetic potential, like a concrete hangar. At the base of the hall the corrugated façade does not, in fact, meet the ground, but concludes in a small, thin ledge and is supported above a colonnade of wedged-shaped, concrete columns. Between these are apertures which open at the level of a gully below. This signals a subterranean theme which is taken up more extensively for the central parts of the complex, and which were largely developed by Zehrfuss. However, here, and visible from the southern perimeter of *avenue de Suffren*, is another aspect of acutely brutalist credentials.

Concrete devices of water management within the gully take on a sculptural and performative expression, complementing the tectonic rhythm of the corrugation. A procession of six water spouts and rain chains project into the gully from the roof scape of a subterranean section of building to the west of the main auditorium, aligning with every second outward fold of the corrugated façade opposite. As with the folded façade, one might equally expect these to be moving parts, capable of pumping, not just statically channelling water. Viewed from this vantage point onto the composition, in this *brut* provision for the movement of water, the language of engineering on the main façade takes on a different potential for allusion beyond itself. The corrugated elevation now appears less a hangar and more concrete dam, the buttress wall for some advanced utility of Parisian water storage and purification.

Andrew Ayers notes that the composition of the UNESCO complex directly influenced another important, late modernist public building, the French Communist Party (PCF) Headquarters (1965–80) by Brazilian architect Oscar Niemeyer, with Paul Chemetov, Jean Deroche and Jean Prouvé. (The long period of construction was due to a five-year pause in the process, as a result of a dispute with neighbouring residents.) Here too is a separation of the main administrative building from a largely subterranean auditorium, which emerges from the ground plane of the complex as a white cupola (of resin-covered and painted concrete), or topographic mound. Strong similarities can also be drawn with the *Fondation Suisse* and *Maison du Brésil*, and Niemeyer had previously worked extensively with both Le Corbusier and Costa in Brazil. Niemeyer had been a member of the Communist Party since 1945, and was in a period of long exile in France following the US-backed military coup in Brazil in 1964.

At the PCF Headquarters we find a mix of materials more reminiscent of the modernism of the *Fondation Suisse* in its combination of the rough and the smooth, the machine-perfected and the raw. Prouvé's smoked glass curtain wall to the main office block dominates the composition on approach, with its minimal aluminium and rubber joints barely visible between the glass plates. Prouvé's long evolution of a relationship between modern design and industrial manufacturing finds a finessed, late career expression here. The façade combines an impression of technocratic functionalism and administrative power, with the architectonic 'play' of an atypical, curvilinear form to the office block, which incorporates a double kink. However, Niemeyer's work is also an architecture of expressive material contrast in which the raw is asserted with an indulgence not present in the earlier modernism. The experience of the PCF Headquarters as one moves through and into closer proximity is one of a material landscape of contradistinctions, an overt celebration of materials 'as found', and which often demarcate powerful transitions in spatial character.

The quite unique use of the sculptural plasticity of concrete in Niemeyer's work in Paris is in its use as a material to remould and reinvent the Parisian ground. In his array of completed works in Brazil, Niemeyer had numerous opportunities to evolve an integration of natural form within his design - anthropomorphic, biological and topographic - and also to respond to open, landscape contexts. The PCF Headquarters is on a constrained, densely urban site on a busy roundabout, but it is also on rising ground, with the office block appearing to sit on the summit of a small hill. Niemeyer's solution was to excavate, to allow for a public esplanade to occupy the front portion of the site, whilst beneath, to provide for four storeys of subterranean accommodation. Meeting rooms, a cafeteria, television studios and parking, are positioned below the main auditorium space and the foyer and exhibition space. This work of excavation allowed for the importation of, what one might qualify as, a conceptual landscape context, in the formation of an artificial topography formed from shaped concrete paving slabs, which augments the topographic character of the existing incline. This is an undulating ground which rises up to meet the steeper incline of the surface extrusion of the auditorium, flattens and then rises up again like a wave to sweep under the concrete slab of the office block. With its final upturn under the office block, this upper part of the esplanade has the quality of a shallow arena, and forms a kind of primal, cave-like shelter under the textured concrete of the angled slab.

My initial understanding of the architectonic relationship of esplanade to office block was that the esplanade sweeps beneath the building to form a plinth for thin slices of pilotis, which support the main block. The impression is that the building hovers above the ground at the summit of the hill, separated from the ground by a small gap, through which one is tempted to crawl. In fact, the concrete of the esplanade extends up to form something more like a collar which wraps around the upper part of four of the building's five pilotis. The principal portion of these four are then revealed within the foyer beneath. The final, fifth piloti is fully freestanding on the outside of the foyer to its western side.

Architectural historians Carlos Eduardo Comas and Marco Almeida have addressed the work of figuration and the play of transposition between the natural and artificial in Niemeyer's work (Comas and Almeida, 2021). One case study they address is the Pampulha Casino and restaurant, part of Niemeyer's Pampulha Modern Ensemble (1940) in the Brazilian city of Belo Horizonte, a drum-shaped building positioned on a man-made promontory projecting into Lake Pampulha. Comas and Almeida describe how the lake becomes part of the total composition of Niemeyer's engagement at the intersection of man-made and natural landscapes, becoming effectively a 'liquid plaza' to the casino. A theme of liquidity returns at the PCF Headquarters, in the expression of the concrete ground as the frozen form of once molten substances, and a similar relationship between topographic and tectonic elements is played out. In this, a certain loss of contradistinction between the pre-existing context and the invented is staged and, as one moves up and through the complex, one transitions seamlessly to arrive on the purely invented portion of the topography with little reason to doubt its authenticity as Parisian ground.

Perhaps the most dramatic detail of this topographic approach is the entrance to the building itself, which comprises a cut in the esplanade at a point at which it turns sharply upward under the slab. The impression of an entrance achieved through descent into the ground is amplified, dramatised. Ayers refers to this as 'sinister' (Ayers, 2004, p.266), which, we might note, aptly resonates with Macarthur's notion of the 'hard picturesque' of brutalism, and need not necessarily be taken as a criticism. I would concur with the 'sinister' nature of the entrance if one prioritises its Latin etymology, as sinister denoting the left-handed, the disposition of the body in its more clumsy aspect, and as augury and portent. For the entrance, although in reality a gradual ramp, is disarming, disorienting and prompts a mild disturbance in the body as one adjusts to subtle, new demands. It is also, as portent, a future-oriented, utopic expression. The reinvention of the form and disposition of entrance is the signal of a transition, not just from interior to exterior, but from old to new social orders: the aspired-for, radical future of the then powerful, French Communist Party.

A similar composition is employed for Niemeyer's *Bourse du Travail* (Labour Exchange) in Bobigny, completed in 1976. This project lacks the level of finesse and attention to detail found at the PCF Headquarters, but also generated one of the most remarkable architectural forms of the era and an architecture of *brut* alterity. Niemeyer worked with the engineers Bérim for the auditorium and public meeting rooms which, as with those at the PCF Headquarters, are accessed via a subterranean foyer. However, here the auditorium does not simply emerge as a discrete, topographical register of the presence of subterranean volumes, but appears as if it were the complete resurfacing of a subterranean entity. If the cupola of the PCF Headquarters could be understood as a picturesque hillock left proud within a once molten flow of liquid landscape, the exterior form of the auditorium of the *Bourse* is more a fusion of the geomorphic and the bestial, which has emphatically arrived at the surface level of public space, and occupies it threateningly, as if it were imminently to expand yet further.

Bérim, which was founded in 1948 by the civil engineer and leading member of the French resistance, Raymond Aubrac, worked only with sketches provided by Niemeyer, and were unable to employ even the limited computational technologies of the time because of the irregularity of the sketched form. The form of the auditorium also posed problems for the achievement of the raw concrete finish specified by Niemeyer. A technical account of the process published shortly after completion explains that an extra layer of sprayed concrete was applied on top of the original layer of the formwork concrete in order to mask repairs made during the construction process. Here, then, is a raw surface, but also cosmetically enhanced; defects in the surface being beyond the acceptable limits of the 'as found'.

Part 6

Reading across brutalist types: the stylistic and ideological diversity of the mid 1970s

This next section charts a series of distinct contributions to the brutalist vocabulary across different building typologies, by the Polish-born, French-trained architect Jacques Kalisz and the French architects Claude Parent and Gérard Grandval. Between these three practices we register the diversity of stylistic expression, constructive technique and ambitions for social programme as French brutalism evolved beyond its earlier dominance by Le Corbusier and the other internationally renowned architects of the post-war period.

Kalisz was a prolific contributor to the expansion of Paris in the later phases of the *Grands Ensembles* projects, with major housing and public and cultural buildings in the areas of Nanterre and Aubervilliers in particular. Kalisz's work is stylistically and materially diverse, but consistently attains to a brutalist dimension through its material expression, in both reinforced concrete and steel frame and panel construction, and in the achievement of an almost graphic legibility of structural and volumetric performance.

Kalisz's Administrative Centre of Pantin (1973), now the National Centre of Dance, has been, since the outset of our project, one of the benchmark projects of Parisian brutalism, and one we have returned to numerous times. The design evolved from Kalisz's diploma project and was realised in collaboration with Jean Perrottet, as Kalisz was not fully qualified at the time of construction. It is positioned along the *canal de L'Ourcq* on the *quai de l'Aisne*, west of the *port de Pantin*. From the canal, its natural typological affiliation would appear to be with that of the concrete warehouse, of which the area has many fine examples. It would certainly be equally convincing as the headquarters for some institution of the port zone – a 'Centre for Inland Navigation and the Parisian Canals', perhaps. It even makes a brief appearance in the aforementioned television series *Engrenages*, being near another of the northerly locations chosen for the scene of a crime.

The original programme of the building amounted to an immensely complex and ambitious centralisation of the administrative departments of Pantin. This included the district court and police headquarters, the labour inspectorate, the municipal morgue and municipal archives, social services, the tax office, the water company offices, trade union headquarters and even an activists' rostrum on the exterior of the building to the west (*Le Nouveau Programme*, 2020). In addition, Kalisz made provision for public exhibition spaces, and spared no spatial expense in the creation of a 19-metre, full-height void for a public atrium on its south side. For this, Kalisz designed one of the most exuberant, interior elements of the brutalist era in Paris, a combined concrete staircase and ramp, which allows for a vertical, architectural promenade through the building, concluding in a landing which gives onto open views across the roof scape of Pantin to the south. This is Kalisz's response to the new concern for social and participatory public space of the period that urban historian Kenny Cupers writes of, an extension of the public realm into the core of public administration and power.

Projecting, rectangular bays dominate the façade on the north elevation facing the canal; whilst on the south elevation, onto the more intimate streetscape of *rue Victor Hugo*, there is a combination of bays and a full-height section of glazed façade at the main entrance to the atrium. The glazing is set in a studied grid of recessed, flush and projecting sections of concrete frame. The form of the building is staggered on this south side, creating a wider expanse of esplanade on the approach to the main entrance. The form of the bays are similar to those used for a later project by Kalisz at the *Hôpital de la Collégiale* (1985) in the 5th *arrondissement*. However, the bays of the administrative centre are also more 'decorative', and were originally intended to be vessels of communication, or signifying 'masks'. The thin, precast concrete panels of their outer-facing sides are assembled into totemic, architectonic motifs, inspired by Aztec patterns. These were to graphically differentiate the principle separation of services within the administrative complex. In this one might detect the combination of the abstract and archaic in the post-surrealist discourse of Breton and Estienne. The marking of the building with a kind of primal graphic continues on the interior with an extensive scheme of mural designs realised in the formation of the formwork for the in-situ concrete. These are also distinctly utopian expressions, of the desire for new forms of communication between the municipality and its public, between the state and the citizen, made possible by a new language of architecture liberated from classical constraints.

By 1997 the building had been returned to the state, after a period of gradual abandonment by the municipality. The repurposing of the building as the National Centre of Dance was completed by Antoinette Robain and Claire Guieysse in 2004 (for which they received the *Prix de l'Équerre d'Argent*), and provides 11 dance studios, a *mediathèque*, cinema, exhibition spaces, offices and cafeteria. Three of the studios are open to the public with the principal performance hall occupying the car parking space of the former police station. Critic Karine Dana describes the intervention as a

work of '*deuxième écriture*' (as opposed to a rewriting); a series of relatively light additions and transformations which allow the original and the new elements of the building to sit in a sympathetic contradistinction (Dana, 2004). These include the strategic addition of aluminium panels on the exterior, which sit flush within Kalisz's original, concrete grid façade, serving to modify the interior views and light conditions for the new functions; a greater opening of transversal views on the ground floor between the main atrium and the canal; the addition of a new interior wall in red stucco, creating a 'curtain' for the new studios; and a programme of coloured fluorescent-tube lighting, inspired by the work of American artist James Turrell. Robain and Guieysse provide a mode of intervention that expresses the current reprogramming of the building as being, itself, modifiable; for an occupation of the building by a new community of ultimately uncertain duration. The process of the building's restoration is still ongoing. Large sections of the bays are currently wrapped in a protective netting whilst a solution is prepared for the concrete rot that has affected a considerable fragmentation of Kalisz's totemic signage.

The staircase and ramp of the main atrium forms, for the community of the Centre of Dance, a monumental 'found object' for appropriation. Its dramatic cantilever and slow inclines support a performativity of the body in public space that both seems like an astute work of anticipation of the building's cultural repurposing, on Kalisz's part, but which is also of a spatial and material generosity that could never be realised in the present for a programme as specific as that of dance.

As a monumental expression of public access and circulation, and also now as a space employed for individual and communal experimental movement, the staircase and ramp design also resonates with the work of one of the more radical, philosophical practices of the brutalist period, that of Claude Parent. During the 1960s Parent undertook, under the name *Architecture Principe*, an interdisciplinary collaboration with the philosopher Paul Virilio, the painter Michel Carrade and the sculptor Morice Lipsi. Amongst their primary spatial and habitational concerns was the development of, what they termed, the 'oblique function', constituting a 'toppling' of the architecture of the right angle toward an architecture of the oblique which would, as Virilio wrote, signal 'the end of the vertical as an axis of elevation, the end of the horizontal as permanent plane' (Parent and Virilio, 1997, p.v). This call to reinvent the fundamental, geometric laws of architecture was directed toward the combining of the solid and the fluid elements of architectural emplacement, to create 'habitable circulation' and 'interior landscapes' of connectivity, which define the individual room and, specifically, the modernist, cellular unit, as a 'micro-ghetto' of isolation. The most celebrated architectural realisation to issue from the collaboration was the concrete church of Saint Bernadette in Nevers (1966). This was closely influenced by the Todt company bunkers of the German army's Atlantic Wall fortifications of World War II; their toppled, inclined, subsiding remains providing powerful, 'ready-made' examples of the architectures they envisaged.

Such ambitions for fundamental spatial evolution and, ultimately, the social, anthropological organisation of urban space, are also echoed in the work of Niemeyer - at least, at the level of spatial and aesthetic production, if not in the production of explicit social thesis - in the complex work of the ground plane and subterranean foyer described previously at the PCF Headquarters; and also in the 'combinatory' geometries of the work of Renaudie and Gailhoustet in Ivry-sur-Seine, which I will return to later. The language of a 'combinatory' architecture - involving a departure from the right angle largely on the horizontal plane - was also adopted by Kalisz for the Nanterre School of Architecture, now abandoned and behind security fences, its radicalism cordoned off as a ruin of future's past.

The curator and theorist Frédéric Migayrou describes the church of Saint Bernadette as exemplary 'of a negative architecture [...] which, in the centre of France, rises up as an architecture of refusal, a repulsive architecture going well beyond the subjectivism of brutalism and the romanticism of an alternative architecture' (Migayrou, 1995, p.149). Our first impressions of a then derelict office block for Social Services by Parent and André Remondet, at the summit of the architecturally eclectic *rue de Mouzaïa* in the 19th *arrondissement*, very much concurred with this notion of an architecture of negativity and repulsion. Migayrou's claim for an architecture of negation moves Parent's church beyond brutalism as merely an alternative, next phase in the onward march of conventional architecture to a yet more radical architecture of revolutionary alterity. Such a claim would only be substantiated by the arrival of the proposed transformation of society through the 'oblique function'. However, Parent's work of the façade at *rue de Mouzaïa* does constitute a quite remarkable avoidance of conventional conceptions of either modern or more historical forms of architectonic beauty, whilst also being a highly complex, crafted and sophisticated work

of design. Its concrete has the thickness of a defensive structure and appears almost like a building in pain: a building in the process of being flayed, with the rhythmic articulation of chunks of concrete flesh peeling back as if to reveal the apertures of fenestration. Bearing an ugly, formwork corrugation, it could be qualified as an ersatz, rusticated façade; an abrasive surface, hostile to anything that might happen to abut against it. When we first encountered it in 2016 in its state of dereliction and with clumsy graffiti across much of the façade, it seemed to have reached its natural state of evolution as an uncompromising example of Macarthur's 'hard picturesque', and what we termed, the 'Bureau of Negation'.

In Autumn 2021, I returned to witness the building's renovation, repurposing and rebranding by CANAL Architecture (Patrick Rubin, Annie le Bot and Antoine Hersant). The office has been renamed *Résidence Mouzaïa* and is now occupied by students, young professionals and artists. Rubin describes a respectful transformation which echoes the approach Robain and Guieysse brought to the work of Kalisz; intervening with a second architectural 'text' that reorients the original toward the perceived needs of the new community. This involved improvements to environmental performance made through additions to the interior, and an aesthetic intervention on the exterior which shifts the semiotics of the building from the technocratic (and Parent's militaristic subtext) toward the domestic. The façade has undergone a simple yet transformational material change in this regard, through the cleansing of its surfaces (including the building's notable work of public art, a poem by Catherine Val cast into a concrete plinth at the base of the building), and the replacement of aluminium window frames with a new, wooden-framed fenestration. Within the interior, the architects preserved elements of graffiti and murals left by squatters and urban artists during the period of the building's official closure.

The windows of the bureau are relatively small, but there are 600 of them across the front and rear façades, which equates to a considerable surface area of wood and which thus takes on a substantial addition to the material palette of the building. Moreover, each unit of the new fenestration is doubled, comprising an inner, rectangular wooden frame, which sits recessed within the deep, concrete aperture, and a second, outer, square frame which sits proud, in the middle of inner frame, thus further increasing the visual presence of the wood. Black-and-white photography does not attest to the impact of the new frames, which achieve, not simply a material warmth in themselves but, in their graphic contradistinction from the concrete, also support a positive, visual reassessment of the detailing of the façade in its entirety.

Such successful repurposing and rehabilitation of a concrete building is also, of course, of considerable environmental benefit, in its maintenance of the huge, embodied energy invested in its initial construction and avoiding the carbon expenditure of a new construction phase. In this sense (and in contrast to the fragile, precast panel section of Kalisz's Administrative Centre), Parent's work seems strategically future-proofed. Whilst not quite of the same order of the indestructible *Flaktürme* anti-aircraft defences of Vienna, Parent's interest in bunker architecture has fortified his buildings for longevity, and the 'Bureau of Negation' has taken its place in the city as a genuinely sedentary architecture.

There are few thematic or aesthetic connections to make between the work of Parent and that of Gérard Grandval. In turning to address Grandval's work at this point in the text, I emphasise the stylistic diversity of concrete architectures in conceptual development and construction in Paris at the same period, with Grandval's well known development *Les Choux de Créteil* (The Cabbages of Créteil) also being completed in 1974. However, both *oeuvres* do support a rejection of the received doctrines of Le Corbusian modernism, and challenge the standardised dimensions and cellular form of the apartment units of the earlier phases of modern construction and the *Grands Ensembles*, albeit through quite radically different paths of spatial philosophy.

Whilst similarities between Grandval's work at Créteil and the work of Aillaud at Nanterre are also, ultimately, limited, the audacity of Grandval's break from a rectilinear architecture in favour of circular geometries and a biomorphic investigation were undoubtedly given an important precedent in the curvilinear housing projects of the earlier phases of Aillaud's career, such as *Les Courtilières* in Pantin (1955–60). However, Grandval was also the beneficiary of an open-minded commission on the part of the mayor of Créteil, Pierre Billotte, a decorated, ex-military officer who also became a minister within the government of Charles de Gaulle in 1966. Billotte gave Grandval the licence to demonstrate that something different is possible: '*Montrez-nous que l'on peut faire autrement*' (Saint-Pierre, 2017 and Chambers, 2021). Grandval's work was also warmly supported by the chief urbanist and architect of the Créteil development, Pierre Dafau, whose Town Hall of Créteil (1973), built for the administrative centre further to the south, is also in the form of cylinder, set on a more formal podium.

Les Choux are a 'brutalist' social media favourite, and an online image search delivers an instant cascade of hundreds of images of this highly photogenic architecture. Their promiscuous relationship with the camera lens undoubtedly derives from the combination of the volumetric generosity of the balconies and their seemingly endless repetition as mass produced elements - a genuinely spectacular combination of industrial production with organic form. Within the online array are a number of images from the time of construction and immediately after completion, including some from the excellent archive/blog of found postcards by the artist and academic Davide Liaudet (archipostcard.blogspot).

One of the most striking and revealing images of *Les Choux* from the period is by Michèle Laurent. It is a Getty-licensed image, dating from 1973, and shows a young couple leaning over the edge of a balcony high up in one of Grandval's ten, high-rise towers. Both dangle their cigarettes into the void, and they duplicate each other's macho nonchalance. The balcony appears a generous protuberance, like the prow of a ship. It is empty other than for small, hanging baskets containing red flowers, which match the male figure's T-shirt. This is an image of a fashionable architecture of hope; no clutter or imported trappings of life required, only being, presence, style, poise. Below, the spread of a new circular urbanism, inspired by the geometries of Sonia Delaunay's 'Rhythm Colour' works, is still ongoing. One of the lower, wider, five-storey rotundas of Grandval's scheme occupies the mid-ground, with its central, hanging garden, and beyond is a cluster of three further, high-rise blocks. To their left are the footprints of other circular buildings yet to be constructed - perhaps a circular garage complex or one of the development's two schools. New, serpentine access roads disappear yet further into the distance. The discourse of the image is that this is a *cité* that could/should expand indefinitely toward the horizon and clear the clutter of the old, rectilinear city in its path.

The balconies, each weighing five tonnes, were the product of a collaboration with the firm EPI Artbéton, and were formed off-site in metal moulds. Grandval had previously experimented with a shell or hull form structure for two prototype chalets for a site in Orléans, but this was his first application of this mode of construction for mass production housing. As architectural journalist Raphaëlle Saint-Pierre explains, the balconies were placed on the axis of dividing walls and although their design was intended to provide wind protection and give privacy (the façade of towers in fact become entirely opaque, obscured behind by the billowing surfaces of the balconies, as one moves beneath), their position also allows for the maintenance of open views from the interior (Saint-Pierre, 2017).

The nomenclature *Les Choux* derives from land use. The area of Créteil was previously dominated by market garden agriculture, and Grandval recounts that there were no historical references within the original site, only the cabbage stalks of a flat agricultural landscape (there was a large sauerkraut factory, the *Choucrouterie Benoist*, nearby). There is probably no single, vegetal reference for the form of the towers and their balconies, but the cabbage stalk itself is a promising starting point as a 'found object' for Grandval's brutalist biomimicry. The notches of cabbage stalks (the scars left from fallen leaves) match very well the shape and staggered rhythm of the balconies (allowing an effective distribution of weight across the superstructure). These negative depressions of the stalk are then, of course, subject to a dramatic, pneumatic swelling to become like architectural organs, expanded volumes, expressing more an image of fecundity, fertility – the pine cone, the corncob, the multi-breasted goddess, Artemis of Ephesus. Indeed, in an interview for the architectural magazine *Le Moniteur*, Grandval commented on how the buildings are '*trés brutale dans ses volumes*', expressing a combination of vegetal and feminine form (Saint-Pierre, 2017). Although the balconies mask structure they do 'perform', one might suggest, a kind of blossoming of the structural system, the concrete frame; they express its performance and capacity.

We found the urban zone of *Les Choux* to be quiet and well-manicured, with a team of municipal workers carrying out landscape maintenance. It had a campus feel to it and, indeed, its grounds converge with those of the *Université Paris 12*, Val-de-Marne. The landscaping is conservative (a more experimental, botanical programme of gardening would be apt here, given the biomorphic themes of Grandval). However, it transitions effectively between different scales, from the small, circular gardens which have developed at the base of some of the towers, within their perimeter fencing; to the intermediate, municipal landscape and *aires de jeux* flowing between them; and then further to the south-west, beyond one of the three major, arterial roads which delimit the site of *Les Choux*, lies the Lake Créteil.

As one moves through the quite exhilarating, visual spectacle of *Les Choux* one catches glimpses of another building on the brutalist itinerary to the north-east, the judiciary or *Palais de Justice* (1978) of Daniel Badani and Pierre Roux-Dorlut. This was an already experienced collaboration, which had developed public and infrastructural buildings in Africa, including the *Palais de Justice* of the former French colonial judiciary of Abidjan, Ivory Coast in 1947. This earlier building is also constructed in concrete, but is a combination of a simpler, earlier modernism with some overtly classical elements, including a monumental portico of six, square, concrete columns. Créteil's *Palais de Justice* stands in almost dialectic counterpoint to everything expressed and embodied in Grandval's work. It is an austere monolith with heavy symbolism expressing vertical hierarchies and the domination of the individual by technocratic, state institutions. Its form is something of a synthesis between the scales of justice and an open book. It is a building of severe symmetries and suggests an urbanism of axial alignments and grand, central boulevards which, thankfully, did not manifest here. Nevertheless, this symbolic projection of the law does impose on the urban experience of the *cité* of *Les Choux* in a quite antisocial and atavistic fashion; a warning to its residents that the more casual and experimental, social attitudes of its moment of conception should not be taken too far.

North

Gymnasium Jules Ladoumègue
Jean Peccoux with engineer Robert Lourdin, 1972
Lourdin's geometries of structural levitation.
20 May 2022, pm: 'found objects': a skip arsenal for the fighting footballers of Pantin.

The Administrative Centre of Pantin (now the National Centre of Dance)

Jacques Kalisz with Jean Perrottet, 1973

Totemic signage and concrete rot; an atrium of promenade and performance: the architectural dialectic of ramp and staircase.

CN
D
CN
D
D

Tour Pleyel (as building site)
Jacques Binoux and Michel Folliasson;
Bernard Favatier and Pierre Herrault, 1973
Chantier Pleyel: temporary epicentre of Paris
brut. 'Found object' of the northern horizon.

GCC
GCC
GCC
JCM

POLICE

Opération Arago
Paul Chemetov with Gérard Liucci, 1975
Chemetov's corner of brutalist projectiles.
30 November 2021, am: territorial gangs; a morning of police sirens on *rue Arago*.

Patinoire de Saint-Ouen

Paul Chemetov with Mateï Beldiman, 1979

Brutalist constructivism; the building as urban accelerator.

4 March 2022, pm: the waiting men of Chemetov's staircases, *place Jean Jaurès*.

Cité Rateau

Jean Renaudie/Atelier Renaudie (lead architect Hugues Marcucci), 1984

Compression, dilation, fragmentation: spatial adventures of the sculpted ground plane. 20 May 2022, am: imposition of a new regime of gated access; abject municipal rejection of the urban 'combinatory'.

POIDS
LOURDS

Cité de la Maladrerie

Renée Gailhoustet, 1986

Late brutalist crenellations of a new 'Fort Aubervilliers': artists' studios at the intersections of public space.

Îlot 8 of the Basilique Urban Development Zone

Renée Gailhoustet, 1986

A medieval urban grain and arcades of the 19th century; visual porosity between commercial and habitational levels.

8h 21h
PHARMACIE
Hôtel de Ville
Stade de France
Sous-Préfecture
VOTRE SUPERMARCHÉ
AFRIQUE - CARAÏBES - OCÉAN
WC

Prefecture and the André Malraux Building, Administrative Centre of Seine-Saint-Denis

Michel Folliasson, 1971

Ark of the new *ville-préfecture*; a metaphysical urban composition.

Hôtel de Ville
Liberté Egalité Fraternité

Town Hall of Bobigny

Marius Depont and Michel Holley, 1974

Precast repetition and filtration: the bone-chain façade.

NOS RETRAITES

Labour Exchange
Oscar Niemeyer, 1976
A topological beast. Building as landscape: fluid transitions to the substratum.
29 October 2016, pm: graffiti (east façade): '*L'odeur lourde de la trahison*'
('The heavy stench of betrayal').

Church of Saint André
Marius Depont, 1980
A nave of tectonic plates and the stained glass of André Gence.

Façade of the Commercial Centre

Marius Depont and Michel Holley, 1974

Rustication in the atomic age; life in the folds.

(To be demolished as part of urban regeneration of Bobigny.)

Concrete Playground

Designer unknown, circa 1973

A brutalist portal; children of '*le hard* French'.

Part 7

An oblique brutalism: the communal, spatial adventures of a 'combinatory' architecture

At *Les Étoiles* (The Stars) within the multi-phased reconstruction of Ivry-sur-Seine town centre, the work of Renée Gailhoustet, Jean Renaudie and Nina Schuch, there are also biological references at play, but at a deeper, organisational level, not simply at the level of form-making. Historian Iréné Scalbert notes Renaudie's interest in molecular biology and the work of the biologist Francois Jacob, toward the evolution of the city as a complex 'combinatory system', 'preventing the dissociation of its different elements' (Scalbert, 2004, p.19). This generates a spatial principle of considerably greater complexity and a very different language of brutal volumetrics. Renaudie's work affects a strong rejection of the tower block and a car dominated urbanism in favour of architecture as a topographic formation, 'something one might climb, rather than enter through', as Scalbert puts it (Scalbert, 2004). Within the work of Renaudie and Gailhoustet it is the complexities of the plan and its social thesis, to be achieved at scale, that dominate the material and constructive regime. The 'honesty' of material expression in relation to structure and the trace of labour is not an absolute value in this work. One might claim, by contrast, that there is a more genuine 'democratisation' of material aesthetics in Renaudie and Gailhoustet's work, by the priority afforded to the pragmatics of the constructive task toward the achievement of hitherto unattained spatial complexity, *en masse*.

Through the vertical layering of a triangulated or 'star-shaped' plan, the vehement rejection of the rectangle and the exploration of the possibilities of the 45° angle, subject to additional morphing actions of cut and rotation, Renaudie and Gailhoustet's architecture accedes to a radical principle of 'difference'. The project is rigorously anti-standardisation. The 'combinatory system' of overlap and interconnection proposes a unique space for every household. Every apartment is different and prioritises the spaces of collective living over provision for the individual, allowing complexity and irregularity within the plan to generate an evolving appropriation of space, from interior to exterior. The work of spatial complexity, variation and interrelationship is ultimately directed toward the aim of facilitating self-management by the inhabitants within the evolution of different patterns of communal encounter and life across the commercial, profession and domestic strata of the *cité*. This also marks a strong ideological departure from the work of Grandval and other exponents of the tower block solution to mass housing - rectilinear or biomorphic - in which internal communal areas were often kept to a minimum, judged to be the spaces most likely to see conflict and difficulties in maintenance.

As Scalbert explains, the 'effect of one apartment configuration upon another necessitated never-ending adjustments' (Scalbert, 2004, p.45). The apartment plans of Ivry reveal the astounding levels of spatial imagination required to hold in mind and work such mutation. Some spaces viewed from public space seem dysfunctional as rooms. They can appear more like a theatrical space; spatial splinters which pierce the normal demarcations of public and private space – the new geometries performing a critical movement from one to the other, in a radical, *brut* rejection of frontality. This also requires new efforts and dispositions of inhabitation, and whilst many have embraced these new, spatial propositions and encounters, a few retreat, with windows obscured, and possessions piled into the acute angles at the limits of domestic space.

Our experience of visiting the interiors in the Jean Hachette and Jean-Baptiste Clément phases in 2018 (which are privately owned), was of families finely adjusted to the irregular forms that dilate and contract across, above and below, and which provide for multiple views, some intimate, some more exposed, to the city beyond. In each case, a glazed double-height space creates a primary point of entry and spatial orientation; a complex hinge and gathering point, which initiates multiple trajectories of spatial extension, that seem to search out the often multiple, exterior terrace gardens. The interiors are composed, less of rooms, as such, than of inhabited corridors of constantly shifting disposition and dimension, and which provide many opportunistic points for emplacement.

The urban project at Ivry is distinct from many of the other peripheral, urban scale developments, in that it involved the redevelopment of an existing town centre, rather than the establishing of a new one. There was already an important legacy of social housing in Ivry, commissioned by successive communist-led town halls and the municipality, such as the monumental concrete and brick apartment block, *Cité Maurice Thorez* (1953) by Henri and Robert Chevallier. Maurice Thorez, a leader of the PCF and deputy prime minister of France 1946–47, is described by Eric Hazan as a 'detestable character', and a 'docile executioner of Stalin's policy'. However, he continues, 'his name remains bound to the memory of a time when, for masses of young people [...] communism had nothing to do with the terrible system that repressed Eastern Europe. It was a world in which fraternal relations were forged by way of meetings, demonstrations, actions conducted joyfully in common' (Hazan, 2018, p.4). Axially aligned with *Cité Maurice Thorez* to the east along *Boulevard de Brandebourg* is the site of the first social housing apartment block in Ivry, the *Cité de l'Insurrection* (1929), designed by Louis Chevallier (father of Henri and Robert). Also in this easterly sector was the *Cité Gagarine*, a similar, but cruder design to the Maurice Thorez building, built in 1963 by the PCF and with Yuri Gagarin himself attending the inauguration. This was destroyed in 2019.

The *Cité Maurice Thorez* was built on the site of the now destroyed clinic and convalescent home where the actor, artist and writer Antonin Artaud spent his final years, arriving there in 1946. The nearby *mediathèque* of Ivry by Nina Schuch (2001) is named after Artaud, an impressive building in steel, but which did not continue the architectural language of the 'combinatory'. During his time at the clinic Artaud was provided with a huge wooden block by the director Doctor Delmas, which, as Stephen Barber recounts, he would strike 'with hammers, pokers and knives, finally reducing it to splinters as he tested the rhythms for the poems he was working on' (Barber, 1993, p.126). We understand Artaud's block to be one of the mythic, *objets perdus* of Parisian brutalism, formed at the intersection of raw materiality, direct bodily action, social and psychic revolt, poetics and abstraction.

The long period of Ivry's redevelopment, from the late 1960s to the mid 1980s, saw a substantial evolution of architectural approach. The project was initiated by the architect and Communist Party member Roland Dubrulle, veteran of earlier *Grands Ensembles* projects, and received consistent support from the head of Ivry's public housing office, Raymonde

Laluque (Scalbert, 2004). The first buildings to be designed were high-rise tower blocks by Gailhoustet working within Dubrulle's office. Five of a planned seven were completed, which are all that remains of Dubrulle's original master plan. Gailhoustet took on the role of chief architect in 1969, at which point Renaudie was also introduced into the project.

The first phase of Renaudie's contribution, and the first building for which the geometric strategies of a properly oblique and combinatory architecture were adopted, was the *Îlot Danielle Casanova* (1972). This is a mixed-use development on the ground-floor level with apartment housing above, rising to nine storeys in places. Its fractal terracing follows the axis of *avenue Danielle Casanova* on its south-west facing façade; whilst to the north-east the *îlot* extends in more exploratory fashion to create an irregular footprint, with sheltered gardens and colonnades. One major wing on this side of the building aligns with the long, rectilinear bar of the south-west wing of the Maurice Thorez building, and the extremities of the two buildings are separated by just a few metres, in one of the dramatic juxtapositions of historical styles and spatial technologies to be found in Ivry. From this point on, Ivry evolved as a town centre in which the zoning of the city according to the separation of domesticity, labour and leisure was incrementally critiqued and eroded through spatial production, to produce a new, medium-rise, high-density architecture: an intense urbanism, but which actively supports notions of engagement, proximity and participation, against the alienating tendencies of earlier modernism.

Renaudie had realised a small apartment housing development for *Électricité de France* to the east of Ivry centre in 1963 with his previous collaborators Pierre Riboulet, Gérard Thurnauer and Jean-Louis Véret of *Atelier Montrouge*, who were also responsible for the 'Little Round Library' in Clamart (1965). These are two rectilinear towers, but of a spatial and tectonic complexity akin to De Stijl-like neo-plasticism, which heralds the qualities of vertical and horizontal interrelationship and overlapping orientation which is taken on and evolved in the new geometries of Ivry centre.

Aspects of Gailhoustet's designs for the tower blocks, particularly the Raspail tower, which includes apartments with half-levels, also indicate an earlier preoccupation with a domestic, spatial provision of complexity.

This was further evolved in the duplex apartments of the Spinoza housing complex (1973), a building which replicates more closely the form of a Le Corbusian *Unité* block, but in the form of a T (echoing the footprint of *Cité Maurice Thorez*). The *Cité Spinoza* possesses a remarkable series of undercroft spaces, with its pilotis being a combination of massive circular columns and a series of shaped, interlocking concrete slabs, forming an architectural promenade of arches and circles for a space of encounter, shelter and opportunistic repose. This registers a theme that proliferates across Ivry town centre: the provision of complex public space of diverse character and dimension, and which takes the complexity invested into the interiors into an ambition for a new, pedestrian urbanism; a realm of communal participation and discovery.

Some of the most complex sections of pedestrian circulation are to be found in two late phases of the development, the *Îlot Le Liégat* by Gailhoustet, and the *Cité du Parc* (both completed in 1982), which involved Nina Schuch and Serge Renaudie (the son of Jean). In an interview, Serge Renaudie recalls that his contribution to the public spaces of Ivry, both spatial and in the use of colour, were in part informed by a period of study in the arcades and porticos of Bologna and, in this, intriguingly shares a reference with the Townscape movement, as formulated in the interwar, editorial campaigns of *The Architectural Review* in the UK. The *Promenée le Liégat* connects alleyways, tunnels and courtyards in an unfolding sequence of intimate public spaces, of shifting acoustic properties and of light and microclimate, with avian realms of open air and the mature vegetation of the terracing above. In an interview given in 2015 from the garden of her apartment in *Le Liégat*, Gailhoustet describes how, in this dense, urban pocket, she is able to garden in response to the actions of nature, of birds, light and wind (Renée Gailhoustet, 2015). The *Cité du Parc*, on the north-eastern limits of the development, bordering the *Parc des Cormailles*, stages a quite remarkable visual and acoustic interrelationship between the Albert Einstein School and the

surrounding housing. Here the sunken playground of the school forms the core of the development, and its full perimeter can be navigated at an upper level via a pedestrian walkway. This is both a relationship of 'overlooking' and of hide-and-seek, with the playground's irregular shape and recesses providing many opportunities for pockets of sheltered play.

The further expansion of the project of a 'combinatory' architecture largely took place in the northern reaches of the communist-controlled town halls and municipalities of Aubervilliers and Saint-Denis, where

Gailhoustet realised major works of similar complexity. Of particular importance within our research has been the smaller development of the *Cité Rateau* (1984) in the commune of La Courneuve. This was designed by Jean Renaudie but realised by *Atelier Renaudie*, which was established by Serge to complete the works of Jean after his death in 1981. La Courneuve was the site of one of the most emblematic of the earlier *Grands Ensembles* housing developments, the *Cité des Quatre Mille* by Henri Delacroix and Clément Tambuté, completed in the mid 1960s. Despite lobbying and the production of a costed and tested strategy to rehabilitate the blocks by the contemporary architects Lacaton & Vassal and Frédéric Druot, the final sections of the *cité* were demolished in 2020. The development had suffered from a long decline of poor maintenance and the impact of changing demographics toward an increasingly fragmented and disaffected population, but the final decision to demolish was also political and reactionary.

The *Cité Rateau*, a project on a much smaller scale, has not faced the prospect of decanting and demolition, but has sadly fallen victim to a recent, major alteration to its ground-floor areas and relationship to the street. The complex presents a dynamic, fragmented cliff face to its main urban interface with *rue Rateau*, whilst, to the rear, the scheme cascades down from seventh to ground floor in the overlapping and constantly shifting orientations of the terracing characteristic of Ivry. The street frontage is deeply incised and hollowed, a space of transitional access to the apartments at ground floor and deck levels, with staircases visible as their own volumetric expressions behind the frame of the outer façade panelling. The volumes of the apartments break beyond this framework at higher level in a stepped rhythm descending to meet the more diminutive housing around it, and anticipating the more complex volumetric arrangements behind.

The ground level of this façade yields a surprising complexity as one journeys through it and extends in places to the depth of something more like an undercroft. Here structure morphs into screen and 'decoration' with columns diversely shaped – splayed and spread as if they were assembled from something like the splintered fragments of the façade panelling system. Staircases and horizontal, first-floor-connecting walkways further fragment the visual field and are, in turn, supported by a smaller, seemingly ad hoc structural system of columns, like concrete props or scaffolding. One cannot help but think that this is a space beyond drawing, beyond specification.

Almost all of the fenestration at the ground level was obscured behind an industrial-grade metal shuttering, and it was unclear what type of space, or combination of spaces, was behind it: domestic, storage, commercial or studio. This complex space of circulation, screen, shelter and structure would seem to provide myriad opportunities for appropriation: for concealment, for the chance encounter or for the ambush; the improvised event and activity, industrious or celebratory, ludic and social; illicit and anti-social. Yet, the space seemed hollowed and left latent. Although suggestive in equal measure of a space of urban deviancy and of architectural festival, it played host to neither.

In a telephone interview with Serge Renaudie in Autumn 2020 he explained to me how the intentions of this complex ground plane as one of animation and exchange were abandoned by the commissioning client, the municipal HLM (social housing department) from the outset, with a planned mix of artists' studios, artisanal workshops and commercial premises never actually finished. Moreover, the lead architect, Hugues Marcucci (who developed the project after initial sketches by Jean Renaudie), left France shortly after the completion of the project and, as a result of a dispute with the French authorities, destroyed all of the drawings for *Cité Rateau*. None remain, according to Serge, neither in the Saint-Denis municipal archives, nor in the practice's own. It was, therefore, left as a space without drawing and, in a sense, without definitive authorship, and has subsequently been drastically redrawn as the result of a recent commission from the *Office Public de l'Habitat* to the architect Rémy Viard.

In returning to the project in 2022 in order to conduct more research in its public spaces, I discovered *Cité Rateau* transformed by an obtrusive regime of gated access, which almost totally prevents the porosity of circulation from the street previously enjoyed. Moreover, some of the most complex sections of the inner parts of the undercroft are now entirely concealed by new, featureless, double-height walls which, in one instance, actually intersects with one of Renaudie's splayed columns, half burying it, making of it a bizarre pilaster. One can understand the need for a modification to the means of access and security in sections of *Cité Rateau*. However, in contrast to the careful interventions of Robain and Guieysse and CANAL Architecture into the work of Kalisz and Parent respectively, Viard's work is very much an *overwriting*, the imposition of a new text, a reactionary and clumsy one, which should be dismantled at the earliest possibility.

As a final site in the itinerary of this text, I return to Ivry-sur-Seine. However, this time not to the town centre, but to a project built further to the north, nearer to the *Porte d'Ivry*. It was developed through a similar architectural language and spatial philosophy to the work of Renaudie and Gailhoustet, but independently of their offices. Iwona Buczkowska completed the mixed-use project *Les Longs Sillons* (The Long Furrows, another historic land use reference) in 1986, and still lives and works within the complex. Like the *Cité Rateau*, this project is a smaller and less well known, late brutalist development, and is more of the nature of a series of connected, in-fill sites, woven within the existing city fabric. I came across it during the COVID lockdown in 2020 when I was travelling vicariously through Paris through the online, illustrated '*balades architecturales*' of *Le Renard Parisien* (jmrenard.wordpress). The complex is represented here with a small photograph of one of the project's corner elevations, taken at the intersection of the quiet back streets of *rue Jules Ferry* and *rue Barbès*, and appears as a seemingly quite minor eruption of the fractal architecture of the 'combinatory'. In visiting the project in person in 2021, I discovered how the project is, in fact, an *îlot* of considerable extent and fascinating complexity, which interjects into the conventional streetscape of Ivry at three different points, with the largest façade facing north to the intersection of the 17th century Ivry windmill (*La Moulin de La Tour*). The development runs in parallel to the *rue Barbès* on an east-west axis, and comprises 96 apartments, offices, shops, a crèche and child welfare services, and a multi-functional meeting space. These are linked by a continuous public space of open gardens and covered walkways. Spiral staircases link to deck access landings and the apartments.

Les Longs Sillons sees the convergence of many important lessons of the brutalist story in Paris and its current situation. As an architectural language learnt from the earlier generation of architects (Gailhoustet, Renaudie and Parent were all important influences in the development of Buczkowska's work), it marks the potential for a continuation of the radical techniques of spatial design of the earlier period and its transition into changing social contexts and building specification. On the other hand, it is clear that Buczkowska, even as resident architect, has faced an uphill battle with local authorities over the quality and frequency of maintenance. The situation for some of Buczkowska's other projects has been more dramatic and distressing. Her remarkable housing project in Le Blanc-Mesnil, Seine-Saint-Denis, an oblique architecture built entirely from wood, completed in 1992, has recently been threatened with demolition and redevelopment by the right-wing town hall. It is clear from this, and the kind of spatial butchery committed at Renaudie's *Cité Rateau*, that the vigilance and protection offered to Paris's brutalism and related works is, at best, uneven.

Visiting Buczkowska's atelier and apartment at *Les Longs Sillons* in May 2022 provided a powerful reminder as to how the architecture of the brutalist period must be understood as one of advanced and subtle domesticity, inhabitation and care, not just of urban image. Buczkowska's apartment stretches across three floors, in a cascade of intimate spaces formed

from the diverse opportunities of the oblique. Bespoke, wooden staircases connect these spaces and serve as vessels of inhabitation and object display in themselves. The limit of the upper, rooftop garden is formed, on one side, by the weathered, side-elevation of a 19th century town house, one of the multiple points of contact between Buczkowska's architecture and the surrounding, historic context. To the north-west of the garden is a view across the *îlot*'s slanted roof scape, reminiscent of the wind-catchers of Hyderabad, with other residents busy in their aerial plots. Yet further, on the urban horizon toward central Paris, beyond the *Porte-d'Ivry*, are the earlier, brutalist *Olympiades* Towers of Holley and Proux (1974), seemingly a world away and product of a more primitive age, of the architecture of the right angle.

LE METROPOLIS
CAFE BISTROT
METRO
Mairie d'Ivry
PIZZERIA
RISTORANTE ITALIANO
AUCUN CHIEN N'A ENVIE D'ÊTRE ATTACHÉ DEVANT UN SUPER-MARCHÉ

East and South-East

Multi-storey Car Park (Le Parking Régional du Mont-Est)

Jacques Kalisz, Roger Salem, Aymeric Zublena, 1977

Brutalist futurism; a double helix as prelude to Bofill's Abraxas.

11 May 2018, pm: *Clos des Aulnes*; staircase to a garden of irises and broken glass.

Towers Raspail, Lénine, Jeanne Hachette, Casanova (also known as Tour des Marronniers)

Renée Gailhoustet, 1968–75

Phares; 'The lighthouses rise up in the city now'. – André Breton, 1932
1 December 2021, am: views from the west, the Cemetery of Saint Pierre and Saint Paul.

Jeanne Hachette Complex

Jean Renaudie, 1975

Life in the folds of the combinatory; 'the stirrings of a refusal' against 'banality and despoliation'. - Jean Renaudie, 1976

c'est bon... Ocb restaurant

Îlot Danielle Casanova

Jean Renaudie, 1972

Architecture as fractal object; origami; a façade for all ages and species.

Jean-Baptiste Clément Building

Jean Renaudie, 1975

A new spatiality of 'qualitative abyss'. - Irénée Scalbert, 2004

Spinoza Building
Renée Gailhoustet, 1973
A new '*Cité de l'Insurrection*': an undercroft of geometric encounter: the portholes of circulatory vessels.

Cité du Parc and The Albert Einstein School

Jean Renaudie, Nina Schuch and Serge Renaudie, 1982–83

The school as urban generator; integrated urbanisms of play and promenade; a children's caravanserai and the wind-catchers of Hyderabad.

Cité Les Longs Sillons

Atelier Iwona Buczkowska, 1986

Open gates to an enclave of complexity; sequential ruptures between façades of the 19th century; scale models at the corner of *Jules Ferry* and *Barbès*.

Cité Voltaire and Place Voltaire
Nina Schuch, 1987
A diversification of the fold, a theatrical splinter between private and public space (intersection of *rue Gabriel Péri* and *place Voltaire*).

Les Terrasses, Apartment Buildings for Électricité de France

Atelier de Montrouge, 1967

Sentinels of the crossroads; a brutalist neo-plasticism.

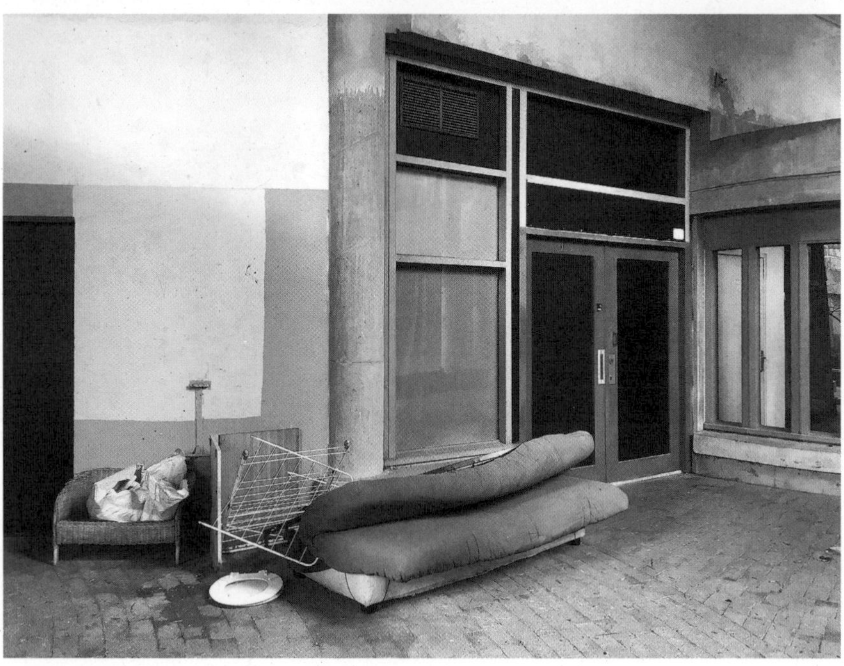

Îlot Le Liégat
Renée Gailhoustet, 1982
Fenestration in blue, green, red (a faded colour palette of late modernity); avian realms of gothic air and creeper.

Les Bleuets

Paul Bossard, 1962

Brutalist rustication and artisanal labour; colour coding and the shifting mosaic of a sun-screen façade.

Les Choux de Créteil

Gérard Grandval, 1974

From monocultural land use to the indeterminate species of brutalist biomimicry; a campus urbanism; life in Delaunay's 'Rhythm Colour' geometries.

Palais de Justice (Law Courts)

Daniel Badani and Pierre Roux-Dorlut, 1978

A bastion of symbolism and symmetry beyond *Les Choux*; vertical city of the Scales of Justice.

Town Hall of Créteil

Pierre Dufau, 1973

Administrators of Lake Créteil; a water tower for the Val-de-Marne.

Maison des Arts et de la Culture André Malraux (MAC)

Jean Faugeron, 1977

Municipal silo of cultural space; ribbed tectonics and amoebic orientations; *brise soleils* for the solar storms of the future.

Backers

Many thanks to the following people for supporting the publication of this book.

A M Stiefvater
Aaron Goldstein
Adam Morris
Adrian Beasley
Agnese Sanvito
Ahmed Bougacha
Alain Mbouche
Alan Boyle
Alan Farmer
Alan Millbrow
Alex Brattell
Alex Filipowicz
Alex Smith
Alex Thomas
Alexis Papineau
Alice Mason
Alison Sidney
Allison Meier
Amanda Gunn
Amy Rose
Ana Maria Dacol
André Meyer-Vitali
Andrew Buckley
Andrew Garcia
Andrew Mead
Andrew Moran
Andy Jamieson
Anna Palutikof
Anthony Gelatka
Antonio B Fletcher
Antonio Chávez Castro
Antreas Tomarides
Argy Megalios
Armin Ganguly
Arnaud Martheleur
Ashley Holdsworth Quinn
Ashley Williams
Babak Kheshti
Barbara Campagna
Barnaby Major
Bart Lindsey
Bart Van der Straeten
Benjamin Cull
Benjamin Lamberton
Benoit Phuez
Brad Jupp
Branko Tkavc
Brian Lobo
Bruno Frenguelli
Bruno Greff
Bryan McConachie
By Eck
Cara Rozell
Carl Arms
Carlo Zampieri
Carlos Traspaderne
Carmen Downing
Caroline van Campen
Celia Cheng
Cesar Giron
Chaïm Eefting
Charles Campbell
Charles Lewis
Chloe Parent
Chris Read
Christian Salas
Christine Navin
Christoph Kern
Christopher Diskin
Christopher Fisher
Christopher Geissler
Christopher Pfiffner
Claire Bruneau-Leblanc
Claude Meyer
Craig Austin
Daan Jenniskens
Damien Guillaume
Dan Northcote-Smith
Dan Vernon
Daniel Barbosa
Daniel Dunham
Darren Paine
Dave Rees
David
David Adam Edelstein
David Bonney
David Keefe
Davith Dara
Dead Ringers Shop
Deane Madsen
Denis Bocquet
Denise Hoyland
Derek Flynn
Derek Pople
Dimosthenis Drivaliaris
Dirk Boon
Dominic Brönnimann
Donald Hankey
Dubois Elisa
Ed Andino
Eli Forta
Ellinor DeGory
Emma Quinn
Emma Reeves
Emmanuelle Morgan
Emmett Scanlon
Fabio Giannattasio
Fabrizio Bianchi
Fariha Yasmin Faruque
Faye Davies
Felicity Mulhall
Felix Lozano
Felix Torkar
Fiona Naylor
Fiona Tchen
Florent Ferrasse
Florent Leroy
Foli Ayivoh
Francis Mougenez
Gabor van der Straten
Geoff Dryvynsyde
Geoff Read
Gillian Lochhead
Giorgio Wetzl
Glyn Taylor
Grandval
Gretchen Moore
Guillermo Lamarca
Hannes Boeker
Heiko Stratmann
Henk Zuidhoek
Hilary Powell
Hilda McEvoy
Howard Kistler
Ian MacMillan
Ian Patterson
Ian Pleace
Ian Pointer
Ingrid Verbanck
Irene Caputo
Isaiah Whisner
Iulia Statica-DuFour
Ivan Diogrik
Jack Cornish
James Alley
James Watson
Jan Karle
Jane Sedgwick
Jannis Weiland
Jason Gardner
Jason Woods
Jayme Morgan
Jean Spiri
Jean-Baptiste Guillot
Jean-Philippe Côté
Jeanne Gang
Jenny Hodgins
Jeroen Loopstra
Jerome Dalmeida
Jesse Hoey
Jia Wong
Jill Miscandlon
Jim Shea
Joanna Cave
Joanna Weaving
Joaquin Fuentes Numancia
John Forgach
John Griffiths
John Grindrod
John Haworth
John Jordan
John Waiton
John Wright
Jon Bennett
Jonathan Davey
Jordan Rodriguez
Jordan Theyel
Jörn Weitz
Jose Trujillo
Joseph Borkowski
Joseph Seliga
Josh Armstrong
Josh Bolitho
Joshua LaPorte
Judy Becker
Julia Brungs
Juraj Kubica
Justin Craib-Cox
Justin Pearson
Kadi Zheng
Karen Willcox
Karin Krochmal

Karin Storzer
Karine Parde
Kate Marsden
Kathryn Munden
Ken Crosland
Kerry Smith
Kevin Ashford
Kevin Maher
Kevin Price
Khaled Matalka
Kim Liu
Kimberley Harris
Kimberley Howarth
Kimmy Clark
Kylie Walker
Laura K
Lawrence Halff
Lee Rodwell
Lesley Mishan
Liam Taylor-Rutterford
Lisa Todd
Liz Dexter
Liza Berdnik
Lucy Read
Luke Beeby
Luke Scofield
Luke Walker
Maddalena Coccagna
Maggie Moran
Mahaley Evans
Manuel F. Herrador Barrios
Marc Armstrong
Marco Barborini
Mare Sheppard
Marek Bašta
Maria Hellström Reimer
Marie Esclozas
Marjorie Plenge
Mark Cassidy
Mark Stringer
Mark Symons
Mark Thornton
Marko Hyvonen
Marko Sillastu
Martin Haines
Martina Jackmuth
Mary Barr
Mary Lamberton
Mary Rasure
Matt Adams
Matt Ash
Matt Neil Hill
Matt Williams
Matthew
Matthew Cobb
Matthew Fuller
Matthew Goulish
Matthew Peck
Matthew Reiter
Matthias Stevens
Meghan Ansbach
Meike Schalk
Melanie Gale
Melissa Kenny
Michael Ageno
Michael Fuller
Michael Paley
Michael Santangelo
Michael Woodcock
Michelle Matthews
Michelle Quaynor
Miles Ranisavljevic
Mircea Lazar
Monica Coffey
Morten Møller Holst
Myron Sullivan
Nandor Mas
Nathan Adams
Nathan Eddy
Ned Collier
Nicholas Evans
Nicole Düpre
Nigel Blackwood
Nigel Finch
Nikki Sims
Nikola Yanev
Oliver Dickinson
Olivier Robin
Olivier Tröndle
Olly Hedgman
Òscar Visús
Paola Camasso
Pascal Greco
Pat Lowe
Patricia Purkiss
Paul Aukett
Paul Beaucourt
Paul Fitzsimmons
Paul Gingold
Paul Goodway
Paul Gunn
Paul Sayers
Paul Templeton
Pavel Bryusov
Pen Mims
Peter Arndt
Peter Lightfoot
Peter Miles
Petr Lindauer
Philippe Albouy
Philippe Bazin
Phillip Bennett-Richards
Pierre-Yves Brest
Postutility
Quentin Loiseaux
Rachel Alabaster
Rachel Carrington
Rachel Stevenson
Rafael Martinez
Raphaëlle Schweke
Refik Gökmen
Renato Pimenta
Richard Newham-Bentley
Richard Rossi
Richard Waltzer
Rick Bleumink
Rick Carlton
Riot Etienne
River Bend Arts
Rob Howes
Robert Pettifer
Robin Gissing
Rollin Salsbery
Romain Guillet
Ross Duncan
Ross Edgar
Rupert Candy
Sally Collier
Sally Griffin
Samantha Smart
Samuel García Vargas
Samuel Karl
Sara Oxton
Sara S
Sarah Whitty
Sebastien Joncoux
Seng Lao
Sheldon Lee
Sigrid Drewsen
Simon Withers
Simon Woods
Siôn Hopes
Siuming Jai
Sofia
Sofia Hård
Spencer McNeil
Spencer Pope
Stanescou
Stefan Kruger
Stefan Tuchila
Stefano
Stefano Ascani
Stephanie White
Stephen Tweed
Stephen Wanta
Steven Gerk
Steven Haw
Steven Wheeler
Stuart Dixon
Susan Schweitzer
Susanne Isa
Tamara Glenny
Tamás Gesztesy
Tammam Salam
Tanya Stevens
Terrence Peterson
The Creative Fund by BackerKit
Thibault Marchand
Tijana Stevanovic
Tim Hayduk
Tim McAlister
Timothy Green
Titouan Benoit
Tobias Künning
Toby Broadhurst
Tom Allewell
Tom Smith
Tomasz Kozlowski
Tony Pratt
Travis Bunt
Urbain du Plessis
Victor Lebrun
Wei Kuang
WhiteClouds
William Arnold
William de Broucker
William Dyson
William H. Glover
William Swislow
Wojtek Hetko
Wyatt Cenac
Yann Graczyk

Bibliography

Agence RVA (2019), 'Créteil: Résidence Les Bleuets. Brutalism à la Française'. Available at www.agencerva.com/projet/creteil-bleuets (Accessed 27 June 2022)

Ayers, A. (2004), The Architecture of Paris. Stuttgart-London: Edition Axel Menges

Banham, R. (1954), 'School at Hunstanton', The Architectural Review, September 1954, pp.148-158

Banham, R. (1955), 'The New Brutalism', The Architectural Review, December 1955, pp.354-361

Barber, S. (1993), Antonin Artaud: Blows and Bombs. London-Boston: Faber and Faber

Breton, A. (1969), Selected Poems (trans. Kenneth White). London: Cape Editions

Buczkowska, I. (1999), Breathing Spaces. Milan: l'Arca Edizioni

Calvo-Salve, M. Á. (2018), 'Influences of the Engineer Pier Luigi Nervi on the Work of Architect Marcel Breuer', Building Knowledge; Construction Histories (6th International Congress on Construction History). Available at www.researchgate.net/publication/333959594 (Accessed 2 June 2022)

'Centre National de la Danse, Pantin', Le Nouveau Programme, Episode 2, 16 September 2020. Available at www.youtube.com/watch?v=0yDgejXJEHc&t=14s (Accessed 1 June 2022)

Chaljub, B. (2018), 'Les Tours Nuages Sacrifiées sur l'Autel de la Performance Thermique', AMC, 267, March 2018, pp.12-15

Chambers, I. (2021), Concrete Paris, Between the Ears, BBC Radio 3. 28 February 2021. Available at www.bbc.co.uk/programmes/m000sqxl (Accessed 15 March 2021)

Cherry, B. and Pevsner, N. (2007), Twentieth Century Architecture No.8, British Modern: Architecture and Design in the 1930s. London: The Twentieth Century Society, pp.12-30

Comas, C.E. and Almeida, M. (2021), 'Grounding Architecture: Unnatural Niemeyer', ZARCH 17 (December 2021), pp.42-69. Available at doi.org/10.26754/ojs_zarch/zarch.2021176128 (Accessed 5 June 2022)

Cupers, K. (2010), 'Designing Social Life: The Urbanism of the Grands Ensembles', Positions (1), pp.94-121

Cupers, K. (2014), The Social Project: Housing Postwar France. University of Minnesota Press

Dana, K. (2004), 'Centre National de la Danse, Pantin', AMC, 143, May 2004, pp.52-59

Engrenages (Spiral), Series 6, Episode 7. Canal+ and BBC Four, 9 October 2017

Forty, F. (2012), Concrete and Culture: A Material History. London: Reaktion Books

Fuentes, J.M. (2018), 'Turning Point at the UNESCO Headquarters. Crossed Influences between Pier Luigi Nervi and Marcel Lajos Breuer.' In CIAB 8. VIII Congreso Internacional de arquitectura blanca. Editorial Universitat Politècnica de València, pp.210-219. Available at riunet.upv.es/handle/10251/107742 (Accessed 4 June 2022)

Harris, S. (2005), 'The Gaulish and the Feudal as Lieux de Mémoire in Post-war French Abstraction', Journal of European Studies, 35 (2), pp.201-20

Hazan, E. (2018), A Walk Through Paris: A Radical Exploration. London: Verso

Hughes, R. (1980), Trouble in Utopia, Shock of the New, Episode 4, BBC Productions with Time Life Films. 21 September 1980

Jameson, F. (1991), Postmodernism. The Cultural Logic of Late Capitalism. London: Verso

Jannière, H. (2010), 'Architecture Criticism: Identifying an Object of Study', OASE, 81, pp.33-55

Kidder Smith, G.E. (1962), The New Architecture of Europe. London: Prentice-Hall International

'Les Choux de Créteil', Le Nouveau Programme, Episode 1. 22 March 2020. Available at www.youtube.com/watch?v=p7Lr8WqHyMM (Accessed 2 June 2022)

Lucan, J. (1989), Tendances de l'Architecture Contemporaine: France, Architecture 1965-88. Milan-Paris: Electa Moniteur

Macarthur, J. (2000), 'Brutalism, Ugliness and the Picturesque Object'. Formulation Fabrication - The Architecture of History: Proceedings of the Seventeenth Annual Conference of the Society of Architectural Historians, Australia and New Zealand, pp.259-66

Macarthur, J. (2005), 'The Nomenclature of Style: Brutalism, Minimalism, Art History and Visual Style in Architecture Journals', Architectural Theory Review, 10:2, pp.100-8

Macarthur, J. (2007), The Picturesque: Architecture, Disgust and Other Irregularities. London: Routledge

Marin, L. (1993), 'Frontiers of Utopia: Past and Present', Critical Inquiry, 19, (Winter), pp.397-420

McCabe, J. (2012), 'Exporting French Crime: The Engrenages/Spiral Dossier', Critical Studies in Television, 7 (2), pp.101-18

Migayrou, F. (1997), 'Manifesto of a Differential Inscription: The Complex of Nevers' in Parent, C. and Virilio, P., Architecture Principe 1966 and 1996. Paris: Les Éditions de l'Imprimeur, pp.148-149

Newsome, W.B. (2004), 'The Rise of the Grands Ensembles: Government, Business, and Housing in Postwar France', The Historian, 6 (4), pp.793-816

Parent, C. and Virilio, P. (1997), Architecture Principe 1966 and 1996. Paris: Les Éditions de l'Imprimeur

Renée Gailhoustet in Interview. Prix Femmes Architectures, 2014, ARVHA, 9 June 2015. Available at www.youtube.com/watch?v=Db-9QM6HVt8 (Accessed 12 June 2022)

'Renée Gailhoustet: Architecte Urbaniste' (by Christian Merlhiot and Jean-Pierre Lefebvre), L'Art de Faire la Ville. Périphérie and La Conseil Générale de la Seine-Saint-Denis (1996). Available at www.youtube.com/watch?v=R73NkGJB45k (Accessed 25 June 2022)

Saint-Pierre, R. (2017), 'Gérard Grandval: Les Choux de Créteil', AMC, no.58, March 2017

Scalbert, I. (2004), A Right to Difference: The Architecture of Jean Renaudie. London: The Architectural Association

Texier, S. (2019), Architecture Brutalistes: Paris et Environs. Paris: Parigramme, Paris

Vidler, A. (2014), 'Smooth and Rough: Tactile Brutalism', in Borden I., Fraser M. and Penner B., (eds) Forty Ways to Think About Architecture: Architectural History and Theory Today. Chichester: John Wiley & Sons, pp.43-47

Index

Fire Station Headquarters and Barracks 24
31 boulevard Masséna, Paris 13e
Prvoslav Popovic and Jean Willerval, 1973
Restoration by AUA Paul Chemetov, 2010
• Accommodation, administration, equipment depot, conference hall, theatre, library, restaurant, swimming pool, gymnasium

Gymnasium Jules Ladoumègue 100
37 route des Petits Ponts, 75019
Jean Peccoux with engineer Robert Lourdin, 1972
• Internal sports arena, stadium terracing

Îlot 8 of the Basilique Urban Development Zone 118
Rue Jean-Jaurès, place Jean-Jaurès, place du Caquet, rue Pierre-Dupont, 93200, Saint-Denis
Renée Gailhoustet, 1986
• Apartment housing, commercial centre, parking

Îlot Danielle Casanova 152
79–81 avenue Danielle Casanova, 94200, Ivry-sur-Seine
Jean Renaudie, 1972
• Apartment housing, retail, crèche, offices, parking

Îlot Le Liégat 168
Rue Gabriel Péri, promenée du Liégat, 94200, Ivry-sur-Seine
Renée Gailhoustet, 1982
• Apartment housing, retail, community spaces, public spaces, parking

Intercommunal Cemetery 64
108 rue de la Porte-de-Trivaux, 92140, Clamart
Robert Auzelle and Ivan Jankovic, 1956
• Reception buildings, sculptural monuments, caretaker's lodge, public toilets, water stations, furnaces, reliquary

Jean-Baptiste Clément Building 154
Rue Jean-Baptiste Clément, rue Raspail, 94200, Ivry-sur-Seine
Jean Renaudie, 1975
• Apartment housing, retail, parking

Jeanne Hachette Complex 148
Avenue Georges Gosnat, rue Raspail, 94200, Ivry-sur-Seine
Jean Renaudie, 1975
• Apartment housing, retail, office, leisure, public spaces, parking

Labour Exchange (monument historique) 124
1 place de la Libération, 93000, Bobigny
Oscar Niemeyer (with the engineering consultants Bérim), 1976
• Offices, public reception hall, conference chamber, multi-purpose room, restaurant

Les Bleuets 170
Rue Chéret, 9400, Créteil
Paul Bossard, 1962
• Apartment housing

Les Choux de Créteil 172
Boulevard Pablo Picasso, 94000, Créteil
Gérard Grandval, 1974
• Apartment housing, elementary school, parking

Les Damiers (The Chequerboards) 74
Passage de Seine, place de Seine and galerie des Damiers, 92400, La Défense, Courbevoie
Michel Folliasson with Jacques Binoux, Abro and Henri Kandjian, 1976
• Apartment housing, retail, offices, parking, public spaces

Les Olympiades Towers 28
Rue de Tolbiac and avenue D'Ivry, Paris 13e
Michel Holley, Jean Chaillet, André Martinat and Michel Proux, 1974
• Apartment housing, commercial centre, offices

Les Orgues de Flandre (Îlot Riquet) 42
67–107 rue de Flandre and
14–24 rue Archereau, Paris 19e
Martin Schultz van Treeck, 1973 and 1980
• Apartment housing, artists' studios, shops, sports facilities, school, retirement home

Les Terrasses, Apartment Buildings for Électricité de France (monument historique) 166
42 boulevard du Colonel-Fabien, 94200, Ivry-sur-Seine
Atelier de Montrouge (Jean Renaudie, Pierre Riboulet, Gérard Thurnauer, Jean-Louis Véret), 1967
Restoration by AUA Paul Chemetov, 2016

Maison des Arts et de la Culture André Malraux (MAC) 182
Place Salvador Allende and place du Général Pierre Billotte, 94000, Créteil
Jean Faugeron, 1977
• Three theatre spaces ('Grand', 'Petit' and 'Satellite'), rehearsal spaces, exhibition spaces, restaurant

Maison du Brésil 20
7 L boulevard Jourdan, la Cité Internationale Universitaire, Paris 14e
Le Corbusier and Lúcio Costa; furniture by Charlotte Perriand and Jean Prouvé, 1959
• Student accommodation, director's house, multi-functional meeting space, exhibition space, library

Maisons Jaoul 69
81 rue de Longchamp, 92200, Neuilly-sur-Seine
Le Corbusier, 1955
• Private housing

Multi-storey Car Park (Le Parking Régional du Mont-Est) 144
Rue du Centre, rue des Arcades, clos des Aulnes, 93610, Noisy-le-Grand
Jacques Kalisz and Roger Salem, Aymeric Zublena, 1977
• 4,000 parking spaces on four levels

Nanterre School of Architecture 70
41 allée Le Corbusier, 92000, Nanterre
Jacques Kalisz and Roger Salem, 1971

Office/Residence Mouzaïa 30
58 rue de Mouzaïa, Paris 19e
Claude Parent and André Remondet, with poet Catherine Val, 1974
Restoration and conversion by CANAL Architecture, 2020
• Previous use: offices for social security
Current use: student and artists' residential building and co-working space

Opération Arago 108
39 rue Arago, 93400, Saint-Ouen
Paul Chemetov with Gérard Liucci, 1975
• Apartment housing, crèche, artists' studios, parking

Palais de Justice (Law Courts) 176
Rue Pasteur Vallery Radot, 94011, Créteil
Daniel Badani and Pierre Roux-Dorlut, 1978

Patinoire de Saint-Ouen 110
4 rue de Docteur Bauer, 93400, Saint-Ouen
Paul Chemetov with Mateï Beldiman, 1979
• Skating rink, parking

Prefecture and the André Malraux Building, Administrative Centre of Seine-Saint-Denis 120
Esplanade Jean Moulin, 93007, Bobigny
Michel Folliasson, 1971
• Departmental archives, treasury and the departments of health and social services

Spinoza Building 156
2–14 avenue Spinoza, 94200, Ivry-sur-Seine
Renée Gailhoustet, 1973
• Apartment housing, retail, community spaces, parking

Sports Centre (Cercle Nautique de France) 78
Île du Pont, 92200, Neuilly-sur-Seine
Albert Grégoire, 1979

Telecommunications Building 22
5 avenue du Général Sarrail, Paris 16e
Pierre Vivien, 1970

Ternes Postal Centre 34
31–35 rue Poncelet, 21-29 rue des Renaudes, Paris 17e
Jean Dumont, 1975
• Offices and telecommunications

The Administrative Centre of Pantin (now the National Centre of Dance) 102
1 rue Victor Hugo, 73507, Pantin
Jacques Kalisz with Jean Perrottet, 1973
Restoration and repurposing by Atelier Robain Guieysse Architectes, 2004
• Previous use: district court, exhibition hall, labour inspectorate, morgue, municipal archives, parking, police headquarters, restaurant, social services, tax office, trade union headquarters and activists' rostrum, water company offices
Current use: offices, library, studios, performance spaces, exhibition spaces, café

The Germaine Tillion College (previously the Vincent d'Indy High School) 44
8 rue Vincent d'Indy, Paris 12e
Claude Parent, 1987

The Little Round Library (monument historique) 68
14 rue de Champagne, Cité de la Plaine, 92140, Clamart
Atelier de Montrouge (Jean Renaudie Pierre Riboulet, Gérard Thurnauer, Jean-Louis Véret), 1965; furniture by Alvar Aalto, Harry Bertoia and Charlotte Perriand, 1965

Tour de Mars 32
35 quai de Grenelle, Front-de-Seine, Paris 15e
Henry Pottier and Michel Proux, 1974
• Apartment housing

Tours Nuages, Cité Pablo Picasso 76
Avenue Pablo Picasso, 92000, Nanterre
Émile Aillaud with Laurence Aillaud and Fabio Riéti, 1978
• Apartment housing

Tour Pleyel (as building site) 106
153 boulevard Anatole, 93200, Seine-Saint-Denis
Jacques Binoux and Michel Folliasson; Bernard Favatier and Pierre Hérrault, 1973
• Commercial offices

Tour Totem 36
57–59 quai de Grenelle, Front-de-Seine, Paris 15e
Michel Andrault and Pierre Parat, with artist Yvette Vincent-Alleaume, 1978
• Apartment housing

Towers Raspail, Lénine, Jeanne Hachette, Casanova (aka Tour des Marronniers) 146
Rue Raspail, avenue Danielle Casanova and avenue Georges Gosnat, 94200, Ivry-sur-Seine
Renée Gailhoustet, 1968-75
· Apartment housing, artists' studios, old peoples' foyer, retail, parking

Town Hall of Bobigny 122
31 avenue du Président Salvador Allende, 93001, Bobigny
Marius Depont and Michel Holley, 1974
· Offices, public reception halls, civil marriage room, chamber of the municipal council

Town Hall of Créteil 178
Place Salvador Allende, 94010, Créteil
Pierre Dufau, 1973

Vision 80 72
1-5 place des Reflets, 92400, La Défense, Courbevoie
Jean-Pierre Jouve, Andrei Frieschlander and Charles Mamfredos, 1973
· Apartment housing